From the Beginning to Alexander the Great

Colin and Sarah McEvedy

CROWELL-COLLIER PRESS

Maps drawn by Kenneth Wass

Design by Sheila Sherwen

Also by Colin McEvedy
The Penguin Atlas of Ancient History
The Penguin Atlas of Medieval History
The Penguin Atlas of Modern History (in preparation)

Library of Congress Catalog Card Number 70–135199

The Macmillan Company
866 Third Avenue
New York, New York 10022

Printed in Great Britain

Cover   The Nile Delta photographed from the Gemini IV spacecraft.
The spacecraft, orbiting 177 kilometers up, was approaching from the northwest: i.e. from the top left-hand corner of
the map on page 20. The contrast between the dark green of the irrigated land in the delta and the pale desert around
is as clear as any map can make it. Note how the two main branches of the Nile have deposited lips of sand at their
mouths and also how the salt has crystallized out of the shallow lakes inside the smooth seaward edge of the delta.

Title-page   Gateway to the second court in the Temple of Nabu at Dur Sharrukin
("Fort Sargon," modern Khorsabad, p. 37).
Like the rest of the town it was built by King Sargon II of Assyria (722–705 BC) who intended Dur Sharrukin to be the
capital of the Assyrian Empire. On either side of the entrance is a band of colored tiles showing a lion, an eagle,
a bull, an olive tree and a plow. The series occurs in other temples and must have had a special meaning. The palm
trees in this drawing are a guess: there were two bronze-bound cedar wood masts on either side of the gateway, but
exactly what happened at the top of them is something archaeologists argue about.

Contents

The maps are all drawn with north at the top except the map of Thebes on page 28

Apes from 30 million years ago to now

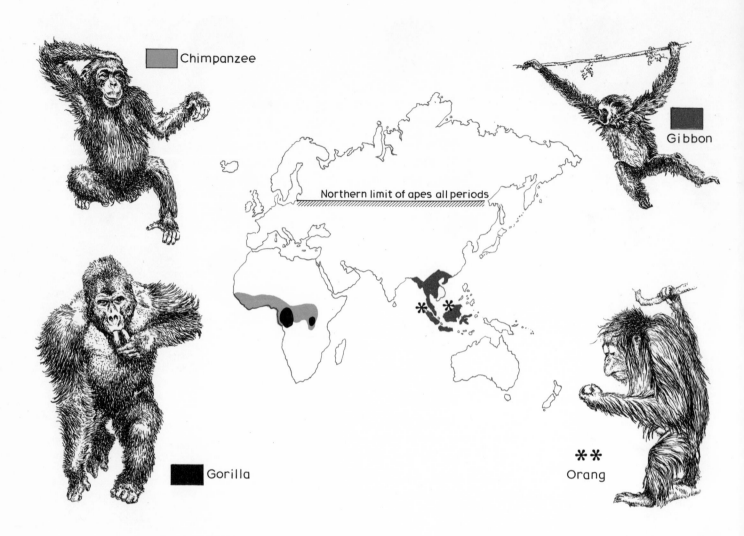

Chimpanzee

Northern limit of apes all periods

Gibbon

Gorilla

Orang

You do not need to have heard of Darwin to see that apes and men are similar. But you do have to know about evolution to say that apes and men must be descended from the same ape-type ancestor. And you have to find some of the missing links between the two before you can say how this happened.

But first the apes, then and now.

Apes are, and always have been, limited to the Old World. There are none (outside captivity) in America. Anatomically they differ from man in having a smaller brain, bigger jaws and a skeleton that is not really built for standing up straight. Apes can stand up and even walk on their hind legs but they are clumsy when they do so and tend to use their knuckles if they are taking more than a few steps.

Apes as big-brained as today's varieties were already in existence 30 million years ago. The only important difference between them and present-day apes is that they were not as good at moving about in trees. If you watch apes – particularly

gibbons – in a zoo, the speed at which they swing along branches is impressive. But how they came by this skill is a story of defeat. Once men or near-men had appeared on the scene the apes could not compete. Only the few who had learned to live in the forest survived.

From them are descended today's apes: the long-armed gibbons and orangs living in eastern Asia and the gorillas and chimpanzees in Africa.

They are herbivorous and so, as explained on page 10, can attain quite high densities (up to 1 gorilla or 4 chimps or 8 gibbons per square kilometer). As chimps and gibbons are widespread animals there are probably several million of each. But there are only about 70,000 gorillas in the world, while orang numbers are down to less than 10,000. Unless they are rigorously protected these two species are likely to become extinct in the near future.

Apemen 3 million years ago

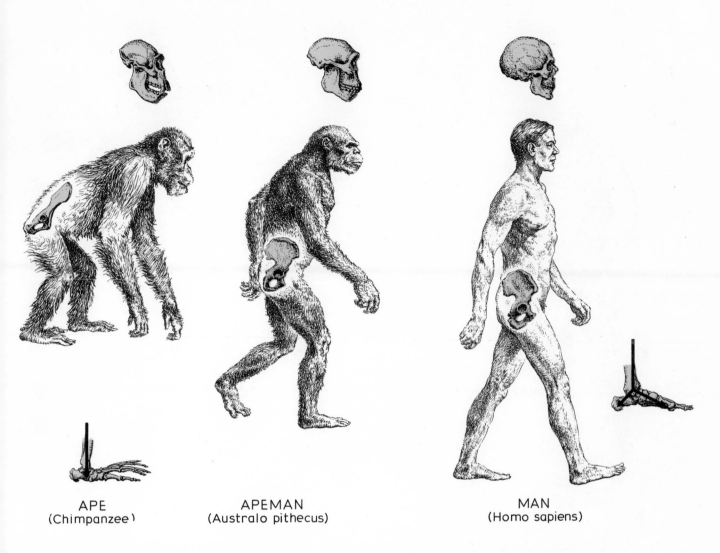

APE
(Chimpanzee)

APEMAN
(Australo pithecus)

MAN
(Homo sapiens)

Bigger brains, nimbler hands and feet made for walking – these are the improvements that make men better than apes in everything except swinging through trees.

Most people would put brains, hands and feet in that order of importance. But that was not the way it happened – you cannot count on having your hands free until you can stand firmly on your feet and there is no point in having a bigger brain if you cannot use your hands.

So in fact it all started with the feet about 3 million years ago when the first apemen, the australopithecines, appeared in Africa. *Australo* means "south," *pithecus* means "ape." They were called "southern apes" because when their remains first came to light in the south of Africa they were thought to be much more like apes than men. It was only with the discovery of hipbones as well as skulls that their true evolutionary position midway between apes and men became apparent.

When you get out of the bath you leave a wet footprint in which the ball and heel are almost separate. An ape's footprint does not have this distinction which is why the ape is unstable when standing up: his weight runs straight down to the ground through his heel. We are stable because the arch of our foot transmits our weight to both ball and heel. The hipbone of Australopithecus shows that he stood upright and could walk, presumably on feet much like ours (a complete skeleton has not yet been found).

Though his skull shows very little improvement on an ape's and he was probably not much brighter, his hands were free. He used them to chip stones to make them sharp-edged – the first time any animal had made a tool. He may even have been able to say a few words.

For a couple of million years australopithecines were a successful form of life throughout Africa. Some anthropologists expect their fossils to be discovered elsewhere in the Old World: it is quite likely that an improved ape would have spread across the whole ape territory.

Early Man 1 million years ago

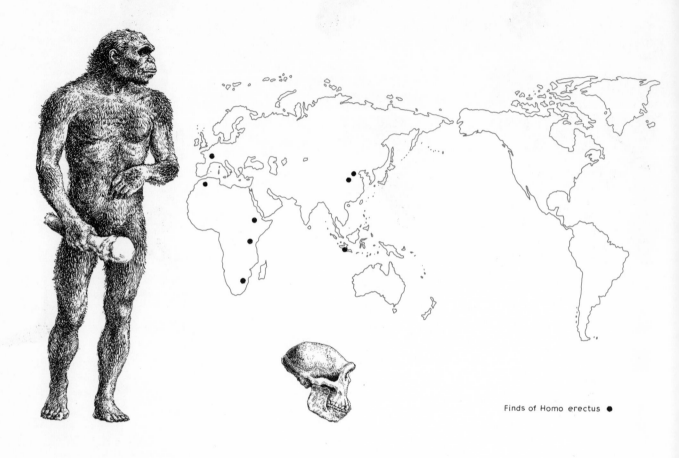

Finds of Homo erectus ●

A brain half as big again (from 600 c.c. to 900 c.c.) changed an australopithecine apeman into a man. Not a very bright or beautiful man but definitely human.

The anthropologists originally called this first man Pithecanthropus (*pithecus* meaning "ape," *anthropus* meaning "man") because, as with the australopithecines, they started by looking at the skull. They decided it was as much like an ape's as a man's and though they soon changed their minds the term "pithecanthropoid" remains alongside the proper scientific name of *Homo erectus*.

Pithecanthropoids have been found across the whole traditional ape territory – in Europe, Africa, China and Java. (It was in Java that the first skull was found 'in 1891.) They made very good flint tools called "handaxes" – though they were not actually used for chopping but for skinning and cutting up animals – and they cooked their meat over fires.

During the pithecanthropoids' heyday between $1\frac{1}{2}$ and $\frac{3}{4}$ million years ago the australopithecines

became extinct, presumably because they could not compete with the brighter newcomers. They may in fact have been disposed of more directly: pithecanthropoids certainly ate each other and are likely to have killed and eaten their weaker kin. Man's first appearance is unlovely in every sense.

Eventually, the pithecanthropoids in their turn went down before a more brainy rival, *Homo sapiens*. The appearance of the *sapiens* species (modern man) is marked by another 50 per cent jump in brain size (from 900 c.c. to 1350 c.c.).

The rest of history is about *Homo sapiens*. But it is worth remembering that the tree-living apes escaped the fate of the australopithecines and pithecanthropoids because (just as tractors and cars are different machines with different functions but a common ancestor) apes and men were no longer in competition.

Homo Sapiens 35,000 BC

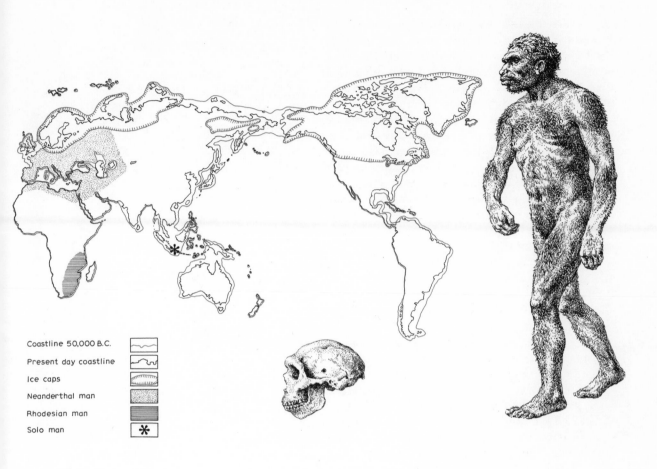

Coastline 50,000 B.C.

Present day coastline

Ice caps

Neanderthal man

Rhodesian man

Solo man

Although *Homo sapiens* (modern man) was certainly in existence half a million years ago we have no real picture of his distribution round the Old World until about 35,000 BC, at the height of the last Ice Age.

At that time Europe and the Near East were inhabited by a race of man, the Neanderthal, now extinct. There were other equally vanished races in southern Africa ("Rhodesian man" – his remains were first found in Rhodesia but he has nothing to do with present-day Rhodesians) and in Indonesia ("Solo man"). These extinct races were more primitive than us in appearance with less chin, more jaw and heavier ridges over their eyes.

As far as brains go the Neanderthalers at least had brains as big as ours; the primitiveness should not be exaggerated. All of them were definitely modern men, just last year's model so to speak.

Ice Ages were a recurrent feature of man's evolutionary period. During them the glaciers that are now confined to the tops of mountain ranges expanded into continuous caps thousands of feet thick. Greenland and Antarctica have icecaps like this now and during the Ice Ages there were caps over northern Europe and Canada. Near the caps the climate was very cold; in areas farther away, like Africa, it just meant more rain than now. Because so much water was locked up in the icecaps the sealevel was lower than today: you could have walked from England to France or from Malaya to Borneo.

The Age of Discovery
20,000 – 10,000 BC

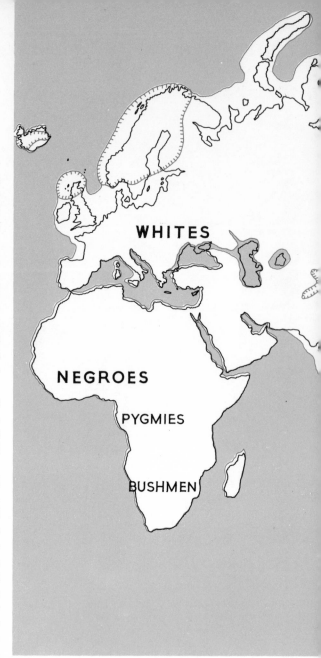

Man's first real success was reaching Australia – something no other land mammal had managed to do. Australia had separated from the other continents when mammals were beginning their evolution and the native Australian varieties were all of the primitive marsupial type.[1]

Of the more advanced placental mammals, only the seal and the bat had succeeded in completing the trip along the Indonesian islands and become Australian animals. Man made the journey about 16,000 BC. Though in relation to human history Australia was to remain an unimportant Stone Age backwater until the coming of Captain Cook, in historical terms the existence of Australians at all was a real triumph.

The Americas are a more important slice of the world than Australia. Despite the existence of a land bridge between Siberia and Alaska at this time, entry into the New World was still blocked by the Canadian icecap.

Not until several thousand years later did warmer weather really go to work on the ice. Then (about 12,000 BC) a corridor opened up and bands of hunters passed through to the American west, where herds of elephant and buffalo provided rich hunting. The spread from the northern continent to the southern was probably almost immediate. Sites at the tip of South America have been dated to 8000 BC and there are probably earlier ones to be found. By 10,000 BC – give or take a thousand years – man had joined the very select band of species that have achieved a world-wide distribution.

The better climate and greater range resulted in an increase of human population to about 5 million at a rough estimate. This is compared to the 1 to 2 million level at which it had stagnated since the time of *Homo erectus*. The new total was the limit as long as man remained simply a hunter.

Any widely distributed animal shows regional variations in appearance and behaviour and man must always have done so. The most obvious distinction in man's case is in skin colour. It may well be that African varieties of *Homo erectus* were darker than those living in Europe because a pigmented skin acts as a protective filter where there is a great deal of sunlight. Certainly we can be sure that by the date of this map men south of the Sahara had black skins and those to the north were whiter.

At the other end of the Old World, in eastern Asia, there was a more gradual change from yellow in the north (with the Mongolian features that are a defense against cold winds) to brown in the south. The Ghanaian, the Italian, the north Chinese and the Indonesian can be taken as examples of what these races looked like at their center points.

Then, as now, much of the human race would have been somewhere between the various types both racially and geographically. The American Indians, for example, seem to have come from an Asiatic zone halfway between whites and yellows.

Various minor races deserve a mention; the Pygmy Negro peoples of the Congo forests and other Pygmies in Southeast Asia, the aboriginal Australians and the Bushmen of South Africa. They are minor races because they have never evolved higher levels of culture and so have been swamped by races who have.

[1] There are two even more primitive egg-laying species.

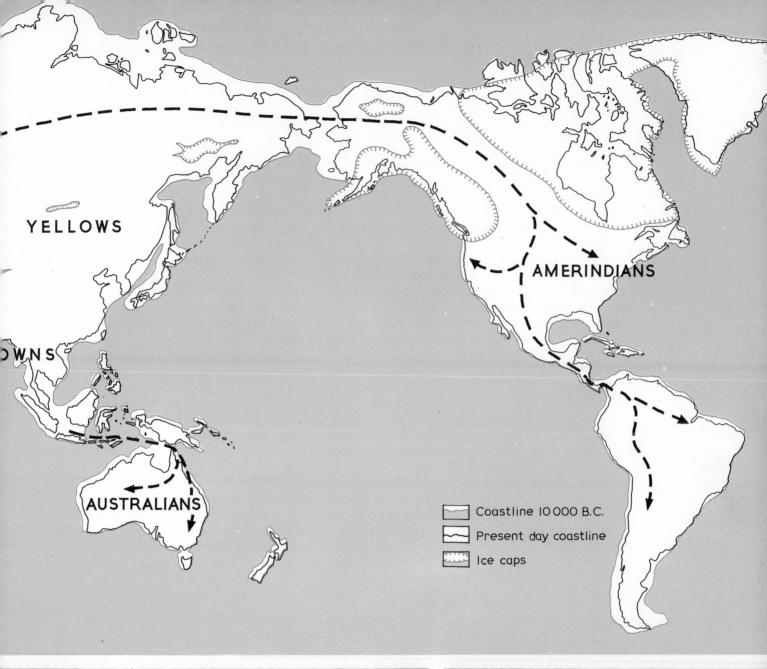

YELLOWS

⟨BR⟩OWNS

AMERINDIANS

AUSTRALIANS

Coastline 10 000 B.C.
Present day coastline
Ice caps

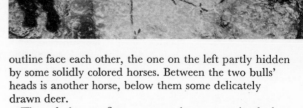

We do not really know when man started to wear clothes and build huts because these things do not last. The only common remains of early man are his flint tools. However, some very early paintings have survived in caves, the best known of which are in France and the best of all at Lascaux. They date from about 13,000 BC.

1 Paintings in the "Great Hall." Two bulls drawn in outline face each other, the one on the left partly hidden by some solidly colored horses. Between the two bulls' heads is another horse, below them some delicately drawn deer.

2 The only human figure among the many animals drawn on the walls of Lascaux. He has apparently speared a bison whose gut is hanging out. He looks none too well himself.

The Neolithic Revolution 6000 BC

Animals get their energy from plants which get *their* energy from the sun. An animal that eats other animals – a carnivore – has simply had his plant-eating done for him.

As the conversion of one meat into another is a wasteful process it takes a large population of herbivores to support a few carnivores and early man, though widespread, was never a common animal in terms of density. Something like 4 people to every ten square kilometers is a high average for man the hunter.

Man was never a pure carnivore but ate anything he could digest including nuts, berries and fruit. By trial and error in times of scarcity, he discovered that the ears of certain grasses growing in the Near East contained edible seed. This seed could be pounded into a flour that could be baked into bread. The discovery took place about 9000 BC and for the next thousand years there were communities in the Near East which lived largely on these grasses (which were of course barley and wheat). This was a very significant discovery because it provided a plentiful food supply at a time when big game – perhaps because of over-hunting, perhaps because the climate was changing – was becoming scarce. Outside the Near East men were having to scavenge for snails and other unattractive forms of food.

The next advance – the deliberate planting of wheat and barley – was even more important, for it tied people to the fields they had planted. Instead of wandering groups of hunters 20 to 200 strong, settled villages with up to 2000 inhabitants now grew up. The maximum density per square kilometer leapt from 0.4 to 10.

This change in the way of life – the first real change in man's history – is called the Neolithic revolution (Neolithic means "New Stone" – there were still no metals in use). It began in the Near East about 8000 BC. The various divisions of the Stone Age that archaeologists use are shown in the diagram below: the only really important one is that between the Paleolithic (Old Stone Age of hunters) and the Neolithic (New Stone Age of farmers).

As well as planting barley and wheat the early Neolithic farmers also domesticated the sheep and the goat. They soon learnt to weave cloth: either linen from the fibre of the flax plant or wool from the hair of the sheep. In time they also domesticated cattle and found out how to make watertight pottery by baking clay vessels in the fire.

The main periods in man's history are the Paleolithic or Old Stone Age (which lasted more than a million years – longer than is shown on the diagram), the Neolithic or New Stone Age (which lasted about 5000 years) and the Age of Metals (which began as the Bronze Age about 5000 years ago).

As well as being used for periods of time these words are also used for stages in man's cultural development. They correspond to the hunting, farming and city-dwelling stages. When Columbus landed in America the world was in the Age of Metals but the Amerindians were not: they were still Neolithic or Mesolithic in culture. The term "Mesolithic" (Middle Stone Age) shows how the two meanings can get muddled; it was originally intended for a period in time between the Paleolithic and Neolithic, it is now used to describe the culture of those who stuck to hunting after the Neolithic invention of agriculture.

The archaeologist divides the Old Stone Age into the Lower Paleolithic (lower means earlier: the farther down something is found in an archaeological dig the older it is), the Middle Paleolithic (associated with the beginning of the last Ice Age and the heyday of Neanderthal man) and the Upper Paleolithic (the period of the cave paintings in France). The period when men were harvesting but not planting wheat is called the proto-Neolithic (primitive Neolithic).

The bottom line in the diagram shows population growth. Because the Old Stone Age lasted so long, the Paleolithic population probably got close to its ceiling of 5 million. The New Stone Age was overtaken by the Bronze Age before its population got anywhere near its ceiling of about 500 million. World population in the present phase of the Age of Metals is about 3.5 billion. The theoretical limit is about 20 billion.

The same sort of fast-rising graph could be drawn for the number of different sorts of tools in use: as man's numbers have risen so has the richness of his culture.

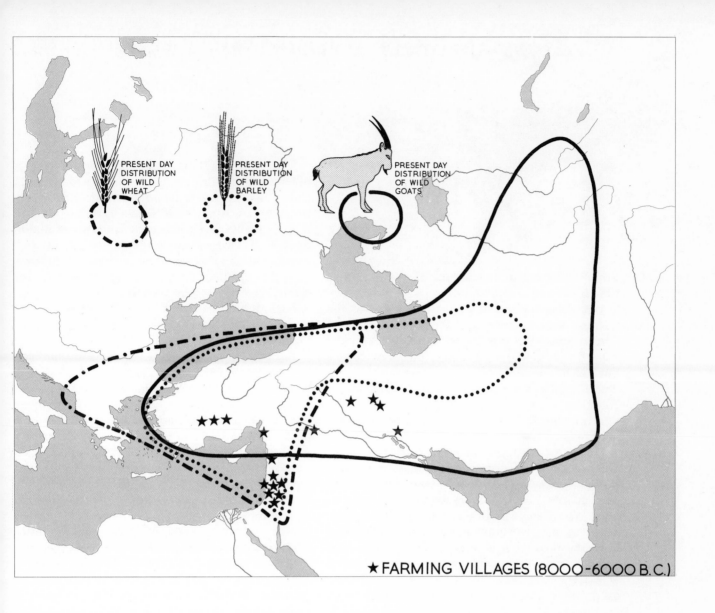

PRESENT DAY
DISTRIBUTION
OF WILD
WHEAT

PRESENT DAY
DISTRIBUTION
OF WILD
BARLEY

PRESENT DAY
DISTRIBUTION
OF WILD
GOATS

★FARMING VILLAGES (8000-6000 B.C.)

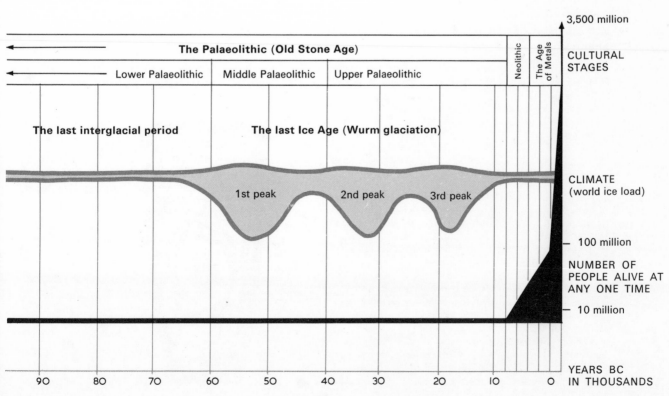

	The Palaeolithic (Old Stone Age)			Neolithic	The Age of Metals	CULTURAL STAGES
	Lower Palaeolithic	Middle Palaeolithic	Upper Palaeolithic			

The last interglacial period

The last Ice Age (Wurm glaciation)

3,500 million

CLIMATE
(world ice load)

1st peak   2nd peak   3rd peak

100 million

NUMBER OF
PEOPLE ALIVE AT
ANY ONE TIME

10 million

YEARS BC
IN THOUSANDS

90   80   70   60   50   40   30   20   10   0

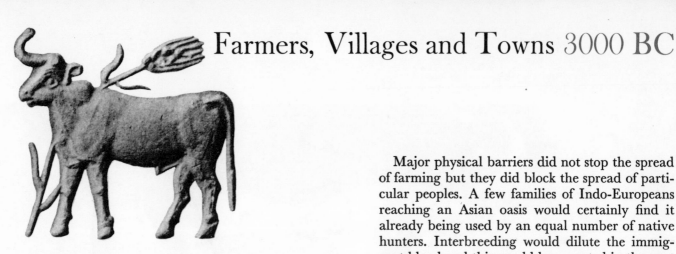

3 Bull and wheat-ear design on a cylinder seal

From the Near East farming spread rapidly across the Old World.

Westward, the spread was easy enough: via the Balkans into Europe, via Egypt to northwest Africa, across the Sahara to the Negroes of the Niger basin. To the south, conditions were harsher but farmers managed to get round the Arabian desert to the Yemen and over the Red Sea to Abyssinia. Eastward, Persia led to India while the Central Asian oases provided seeding points on the long road to China.

Unless the need for water tied them to a particular spot early farmers tended to move frequently – it was easier to clear new ground (by burning) than maintain the fertility of old fields (by manuring). Within any sizeable arable area the spread was consequently rapid and the farmers must soon have absorbed the few hunters in their path.

In Europe the people who carried farming across the Continent were Indo-Europeans, the group from which nearly all Europeans of today are descended. In North Africa they were Hamites, a group that consists of the Berbers, Egyptians and Abyssinians and has a common origin in the Semites of Arabia.[1]

Major physical barriers did not stop the spread of farming but they did block the spread of particular peoples. A few families of Indo-Europeans reaching an Asian oasis would certainly find it already being used by an equal number of native hunters. Interbreeding would dilute the immigrant blood and this would be repeated in the next generation at the next oasis. By the time Asia was crossed the pioneers were Asian. In this way the Sahara, the Hindu Kush and the vastness of Asia preserved the blacks, browns and yellows from white infiltration.

Agriculture prospers best where strong sunlight and abundant fresh water exist: a river crossing a desert is the perfect combination. Even now the Nile, Tigris and Euphrates support rural populations far denser than those of countries that rely on rainfall and a paler sun. The early settlements in these river valleys are of great importance because they were permanent. In time they outgrew the status of villages (up to 5000 inhabitants) and became towns (with 5000 to 15,000 inhabitants).

The appearance of these larger communities allowed a man to specialize and encouraged the society to organize more effectively. In place of the chief, the heads of families, the itinerant tinker and the medicine man we find the king, the council, the craftsman and the priest. And, taking note of it all, the scribe.

[1] The third main group of whites, the Caucasians, to the north and east of the original farming zone, hardly spread out at all.

4 The commonest find in an archaeological dig is a piece of broken pottery. Because fashions in pottery change, an archaeologist can often date a community fairly accurately just by looking at a few pottery fragments. A particular shape or decorative style signposts a particular people and time.

Pottery was invented at an early stage in the spread of farming: to a large extent the two go together. So the archaeologist uses pottery to classify early farming communities – he talks of "beaker folk" and "painted pottery people."

The pot illustrated was found at Susa in Persia and dates from about 3000 BC. It is decorated with stylised animals – giraffe-like creatures round the rim, a strip of what look like wolves and then goats with exaggerated horns.

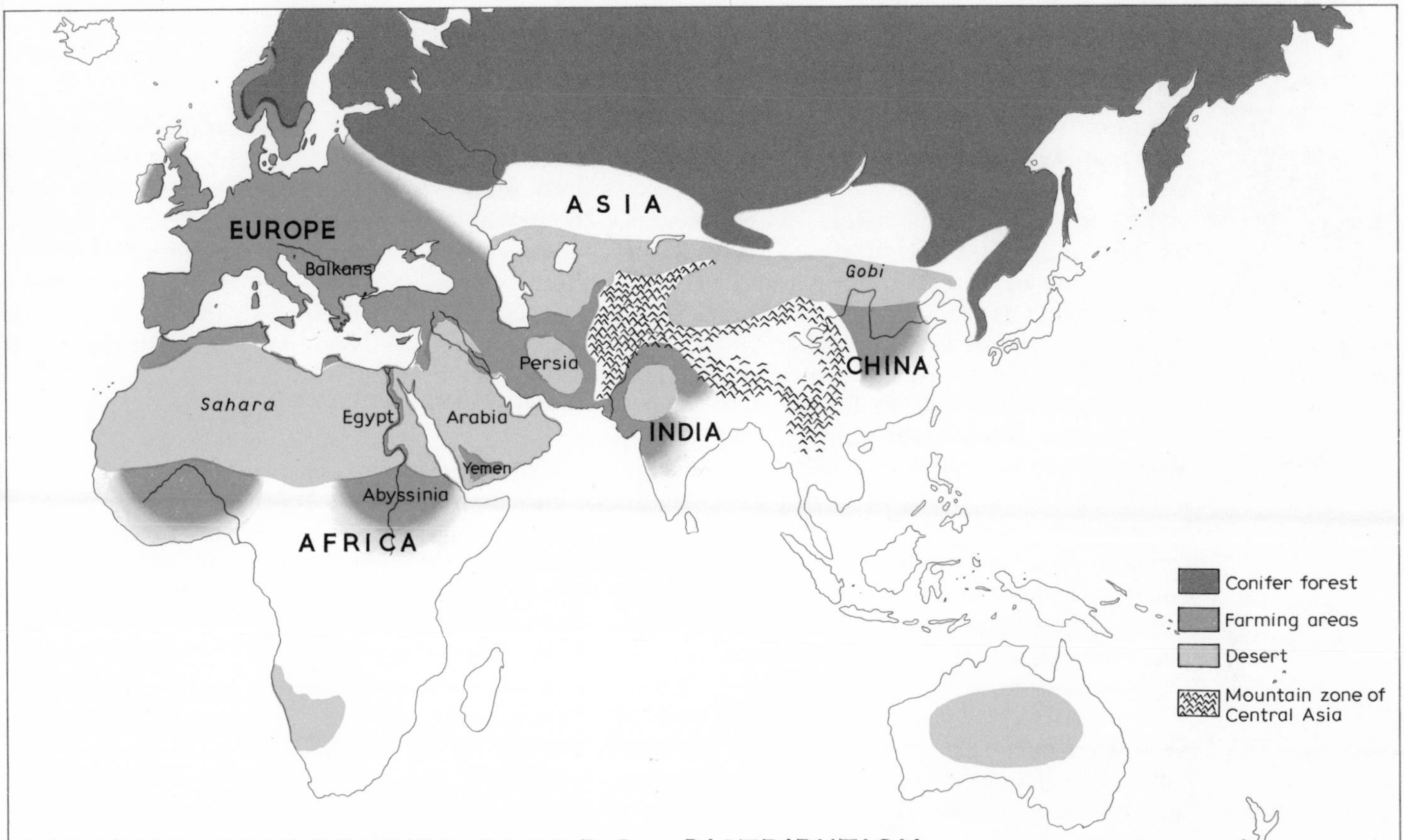
EUROPE
ASIA
Balkans
Gobi
Persia
CHINA
Sahara
Egypt
Arabia
INDIA
Yemen
Abyssinia
AFRICA
Conifer forest
Farming areas
Desert
Mountain zone of Central Asia

FARMING COMMUNITIES 3000 B.C.—DISTRIBUTION

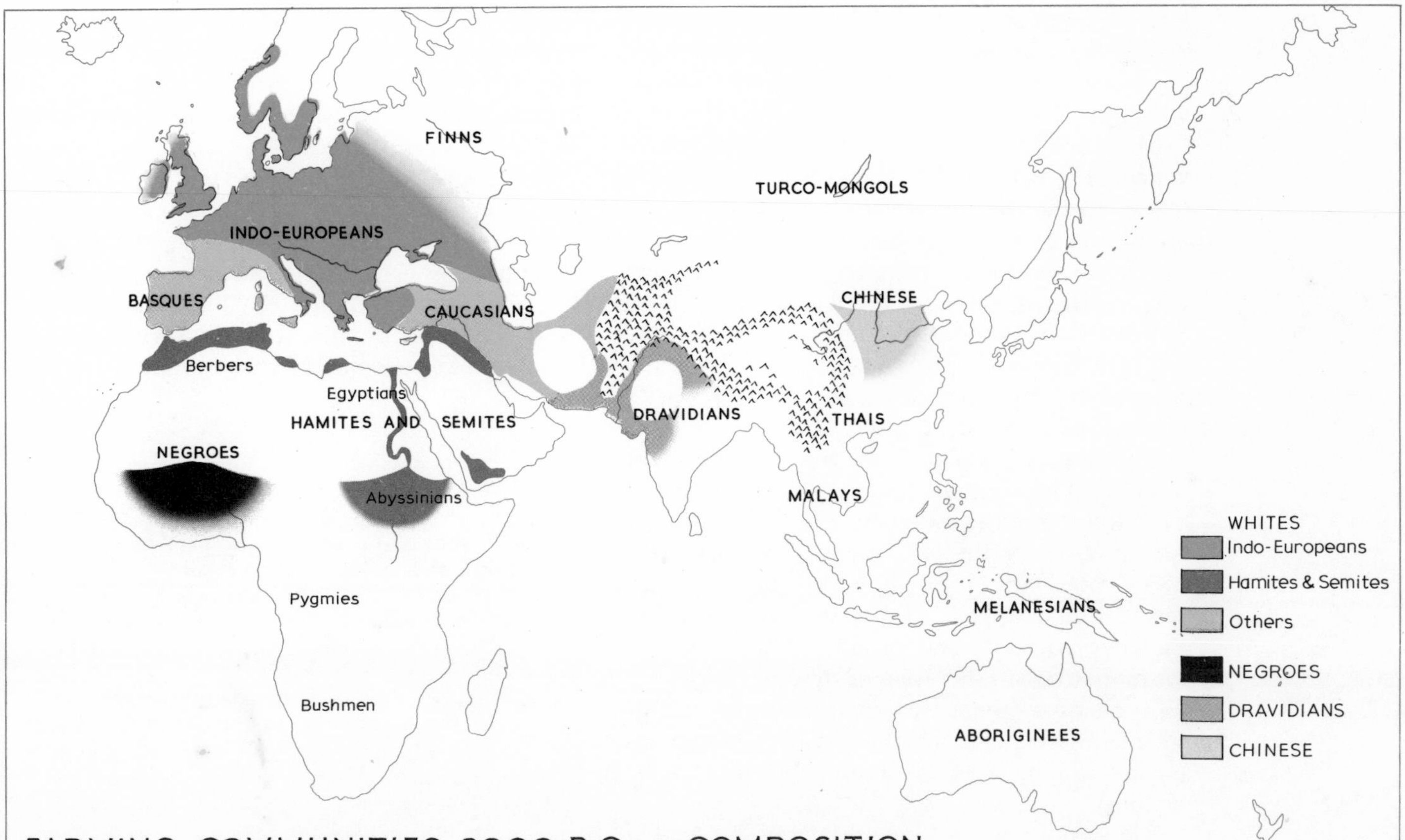
FINNS
TURCO-MONGOLS
INDO-EUROPEANS
BASQUES
CAUCASIANS
CHINESE
Berbers
Egyptians
HAMITES AND SEMITES
DRAVIDIANS
THAIS
NEGROES
Abyssinians
MALAYS
Pygmies
MELANESIANS
Bushmen
ABORIGINEES
WHITES
Indo-Europeans
Hamites & Semites
Others
NEGROES
DRAVIDIANS
CHINESE

FARMING COMMUNITIES 3000 B.C.— COMPOSITION

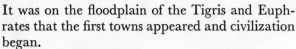

The Sumerians 3000 – 2000 BC

It was on the floodplain of the Tigris and Euphrates that the first towns appeared and civilization began.

This area is the southernmost part of the country known in Classical times as Mesopotamia (Mesopotamia is Greek for "between the rivers") and nowadays as Iraq. Its first inhabitants called it Sumer so we call them Sumerians.

The Sumerian towns are shown on the map over the page. They are often called cities because each was an independent political unit with its own king and its special god. But by present-day standards they would hardly qualify as towns, the biggest having perhaps 20,000 inhabitants. "City" conjures up altogether too grand a picture. The houses were built of mud-brick, as were the town walls, the temples and the ziggurat – a step-pyramid with a temple at the top which was the pride of every town.

The prosperity of Sumer depended on its irrigated fields: the creation (*c.* 4000 BC) and collapse (*c.* 2000 BC) of the irrigation system mark the beginning and end of Sumerian history.

The inventions of the period include all the techniques necessary for a civilized life: metal-working (bronze but not iron), the potter's wheel, the wheeled cart and a script that was a genuine form of literacy and not merely picture-writing.

Metal-working involves several techniques to which different peoples probably contributed: it seems likely the Sumerians' contribution was important since bronze first appears in the Near East when Sumer was prospering. With the wheel and writing we know we are dealing with purely Sumerian inventions. All later examples derive from the Sumerian prototypes. This is enough to secure this long-vanished people their place at the head of history's first chapter.

Techniques apart, Sumerian history lacks interest. The various towns quarrelled, mostly over water rights, and their kings led armies of spearmen to battle with each other. Success in battle conferred prestige and other disputing towns would appeal to a victorious king. This shadowy authority was rarely kept by any town for more than a generation or two.

In 2250 BC Sumer was finally unified – but not by a Sumerian. Sargon the Great, the man who created the first Mesopotamian Empire, was a Semite.

The Semites were the herdsmen of the Arabian peninsula and the farmers of its oases: in one sense Sumer was just a very big oasis on the northeast edge of their territory. Semites had always filtered into Sumer and by Sargon's time they were dominant in the northern part of Sumer (this now became known as Akkad). Sargon advanced his frontier not only south over Sumeria, but north through Assyria and Syria to the Mediterranean and Anatolia. His empire lasted through his grandson's time but was then overthrown by an invasion of hill tribes from the Zagros mountain range.

The Zagros overlooks Iraq on the east and forms the edge of the Iranian (Persian) plateau. Since the time of Sargon Mesopotamia has often been a battleground when the powers of the Iranian plateau have swept down from the Zagros upon the Semites of Arabia.

But before this pattern set in the Sumerians had one more century of independence. The Sumerian kings of Ur cleared out the hillsmen, re-established the frontiers and gave Sumer's final years both peace and honor.

However, the strength of Sumer was ebbing fast: centuries of irrigation had gradually raised the water table (the level of the underground water) until this was touching the roots of the crops. The underground water is loaded with salt and salt kills plants. By 2000 BC it had become impossible to grow wheat in Sumer and barley yields had been halved.

Impoverished and depopulated, the Empire of Ur collapsed under the combined assault of Semite and Zagros tribes. The center of Mesopotamian power moved permanently north to Babylon. The remnant of the Sumerians was absorbed by the Semites who have ever since been the dominant people of Mesopotamia.

5 Soldier of Ur.

6 Air photograph of the town of Erbil in Iraq.

Mud-brick houses have a short life. As new houses are constantly being built on the debris of the old, the level of a mud-brick town rises steadily. Consequently the town ends up on a high mound – not necessarily a bad thing as the town is then easier to defend against enemies and floods.

Modern Erbil shows the process in an advanced stage: it is after all 3000 years old, being the ancient Arbela of Assyria.

If you ignore the buildings outside the walls the Mesopotamian town of Sumerian times must have looked very much like this though in place of the mosque (the building with pimple domes near the town centre) you must picture a ziggurat.

7 Ziggurat of Ur.

The lower stage of this three-step pyramid has recently been restored to its original appearance. So has the triple staircase leading up to the ruined second stage. For a guess at what the complete ziggurat looked like turn to page 21.

The biggest ziggurat was a seven-story one at Babylon which was the origin of the Biblical story of the Tower of Babel.

8 Gudea, Governor of Lagash under the kings of Ur.

9 Bronze head of an Akkadian ruler, usually supposed to be Sargon the Great.

Bronze is made by adding tin to copper (10 per cent tin and 90 per cent copper). It is much harder than either tin or copper and much easier to cast. Indeed, neither metal is much use on its own for either tools or weapons.

The head is about three-quarters life-size.

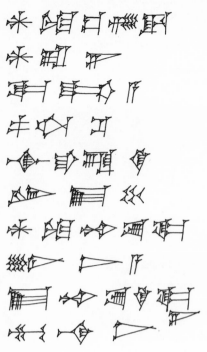

	dingir nin-giz-zi-da	The god "Lord Gizzida"
	dingir-ra-ni	the god of
	gu-de-a	Gudea
	en-si	governor
	lagasa-ki	of Lagash
	lu e-ninnu	(the man who the "Temple of 50"
	dingir nin-gir-su-ka	of the god "Lord of Lagash"
	in-du-a	built)
	e gir-su-ki-ka-ni	his temple in Lagash
	mu-na-du	he built for him.

10 Building inscription of Gudea, Governor of Lagash, with a drawing of the inscription, a transcription into our alphabet and a literal translation.

The meaning is: "Gudea, Governor of Lagash, who built the 'Temple of 50' of the god 'Lord of Lagash', built this temple for the god 'Lord Gizzida' in Lagash."

SUMERIAN WRITING

Sumerians wrote on clay. In place of a pen they used a reed with the end cut to make a wedge-shaped mark on the clay. Each sign consisted of a series of these wedge marks in a particular pattern. Writing of this sort is called "cuneiform" (meaning "wedge-shaped") and many peoples – the Akkadians, Assyrians and Hittites among them – copied this Sumerian style. In fact it continued in use long after the Sumerians were forgotten, only dying out at the beginning of the Christian era.

As you might expect the Sumerian system evolved from picture-writing. The pictures were soon simplified for the sake of speed and by Gudea's time were no longer easily recognizable. For example, it is difficult to see that the first sign in the last but one line above is a picture of a house, but that is what it probably is.

Many words are hard to express in pictures. House is easy enough, but what about God? The Sumerians used a star as their sign for God, an example of a symbolic picture. However, the only answer in the long run was to build up words phonetically (sound by sound). So the Sumerians would use their sign for "sword" which was pronounced "gir," whenever the sound "gir" occurred. It is used in this phonetic way in the last but one line, as part of a word that has nothing to do with swords. The equivalent in English would be to write disorder as (dis)- † -(er).

◀ 11 Early Sumerian tablet. Dating from about 3000 BC, this is an account of fields and their crops. It is only one stage better than a tally and the style of writing lacks the cuneiform appearance of later, more evolved inscriptions like Gudea's.

12 Cuneiform writing at its most perfect. An inscription of the Assyrian king Sennacherib (705–680 BC) giving an account of his campaigns, including one against King Hezekiah of Judah. Found at Nineveh. ▶

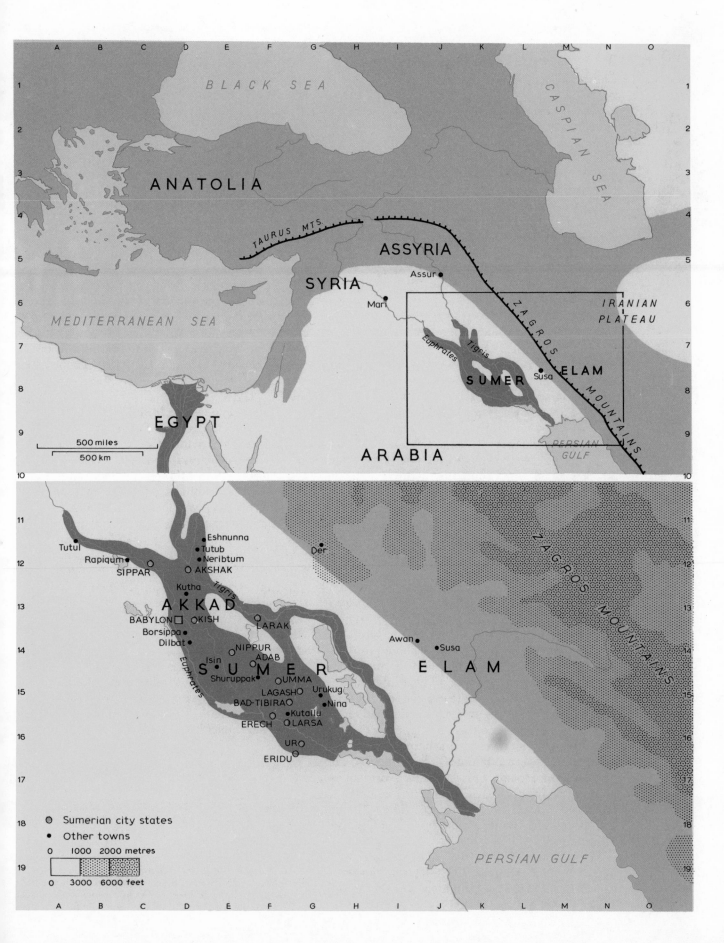

Upper map labels:

BLACK SEA

CASPIAN SEA

ANATOLIA

TAURUS MTS.

ASSYRIA

Assur

SYRIA

Mari

MEDITERRANEAN SEA

Euphrates

Tigris

ZAGROS

IRANIAN PLATEAU

ELAM

SUMER

Susa

MOUNTAINS

EGYPT

ARABIA

PERSIAN GULF

500 miles

500 km

Lower map labels:

Tutul

Rapiqum

SIPPAR

Eshnunna

Tutub

Neribtum

AKSHAK

Der

Kutha

Tigris

AKKAD

BABYLON☐ ○KISH

LARAK

ZAGROS MOUNTAINS

Borsippa

Dilbat

NIPPUR

ADAB

Awan

Susa

Euphrates

S U M E R

Isin

ELAM

Shuruppak

UMMA

LAGASH○

Urukug

BAD-TIBIRA○

Nina

Kutallu

ERECH ○LARSA

UR○

ERIDU ○

○ Sumerian city states

● Other towns

0   1000   2000 metres

0   3000   6000 feet

PERSIAN GULF

17

Egypt 3000 – 1800 BC

13 Egyptian soldier.

The twin rivers of Sumer gave the country breadth as well as length. Their natural overflow, plus a network of canals, made it possible to cultivate most of the area between them. Egypt, on the other hand, has length (1000 kilometers) but almost no breadth (on average, 15 kilometers).

The country consists of villages strung along the Nile like beads – on either side is arid desert. The fertile strip expands in two places: the area now known as the Fayum where a branch of the Nile goes off to a dead-end lake and, more important, the Delta. The Delta was known in ancient times as Lower Egypt because it was downstream. It has as much arable land as the whole of the rest of Egypt.

One might think that this area, tightly packed with settlements, would be more likely to produce an effective political unit than thin and straggling Upper Egypt. But in fact it was Upper Egypt that united first and an Upper Egyptian king who conquered the Delta and became the first "Pharaoh of the Two Lands" (Upper and Lower Egypt).

This is not so surprising if we remember that until very recently it was easier to travel by water than by land – so the villages of Upper Egypt were all positioned on a unifying highway. In the Delta, as in Sumer, the waterways were a help in one direction but made cross-country progress difficult: union did not come naturally. Besides, at this stage (3000 BC) much of the Delta was still marshland; it was only gradually developed over the next 2000 years.

Egypt's peculiar geography had another important historical effect: isolation. The country is effectively an island, surrounded by desert. Though the Nile flows to the sea, the lakes and marshes along the Delta coast are contaminated with salt sea-water and the ground is useless for agriculture. The villages are all well inland.

This barren coast sealed the Egyptians into the Nile Valley, cut them off from outside influences and allowed their culture to continue almost unchanged for 3000 years. It is hard to detect any difference between a temple built in 2000 BC and one built in 200 BC. On the walls are identical gatherings of gods receiving the homage of apparently identical pharaohs. The Ancient World moved slowly: Ancient Egypt barely moved at all.

Menes, the unifier of the country, came from Thinis in Upper Egypt. Once he was master of Lower Egypt as well he built himself a new capital. This was Memphis, appropriately situated at the apex of the Delta. For the whole period known as the Old Kingdom (roughly 3000 – 2200 BC) the pharaohs ruled Egypt from Memphis.

Egyptian rulers are grouped in dynasties. Each consists of half a dozen pharaohs, supposedly of the same family. On average a dynasty lasted something over a hundred years. During the Old Kingdom six dynasties ruled Egypt. Nothing is known of the first two except the names of the pharaohs, for the other four we have names and pyramids (page 21).

The First Intermediate Period which followed the Sixth Dynasty lasted for two centuries. During this time there were two dynasties of pharaohs at Heracleopolis, recognized by the middle third of Egypt but not by the Delta or the southern third of the country. Eventually a Theban noble set himself up as a rival pharaoh and, after a period of equilibrium between the two, Thebes beat Heracleopolis and the country was united once more.

The next phase is the Middle Kingdom (2000 – 1800 BC, the Twelfth and Thirteenth Dynasties[1]). Once again the victor came from the south and founded a new capital in the north, this time at Lisht, just south of Memphis. There is a bit more history to the Middle Kingdom than to the Old. Egyptian armies pushed up to the Second Cataract and made it the south frontier of the country, Egyptian ships visited the coast of Palestine and Syria and brought back the timber Egypt lacked, others sailed the Red Sea as far as "Punt" (the Yemen?) to get incense for the many temples of their homeland. But none of these expeditions really altered anything. To the Egyptian, Egypt was the world and non-Egyptians were of no interest.

In 1800 BC the central authority collapsed again. The Second Intermediate Period began with separate dynasties ruling from Xois in the Delta (Fourteenth Dynasty) and Thebes in the south (Seventeenth Dynasty).

[1] The Seventh and Eighth Dynasties cover the collapse of Memphite rule, the Ninth and Tenth Dynasties are the Heracleopolitan pharaohs and the Eleventh Dynasty consists of the Theban rulers up to the overthrow of the Heracleopolitans.

EGYPTIAN WRITING

The sentence above is taken from the autobiography of a Middle Kingdom official. It means, "I spent many years in the service of His Majesty the Immortal Falcon-god, the King of Lower and Upper Egypt, the Pharaoh Saraintef."

The papyrus reed and the bee in line 11 are symbols of the two kingdoms of Egypt. The pharaoh's name was always enclosed in the special oval now known as a "cartouche" – this fact was a great help in deciphering the script.

The signs represented by an asterisk in column 2 are not meant to be pronounced, they merely serve as clues to the meaning of the words. The circle with a dot in it in line 2, for example, is a sun and means that the word is concerned with time. These clues (called "determinatives") are necessary because the signs often have several meanings. The sun sign appears again in line 12 but on this occasion it means Ra, the sun god. The whole system is very similar to Sumerian and undoubtedly derives from it.

Like the example here, most surviving Egyptian inscriptions are in hieroglyphs on stone. But the ordinary way of writing was with a brush and ink on a paper-like material made from the papyrus reed. An early example of this is the fragment of papyrus below (16). The heading (on the left) is in painted hieroglyphics, the main text (on the right) in a much simplified hieroglyphic script called "hieratic."

A beautiful example of hieratic from a much later period – Twentieth Dynasty as opposed to Fifth Dynasty – is illustrated below (17). It enumerates the gifts made by Rameses III to various temples and is part of a long scroll found at Medinet Habu.

	i-u-$\frac{ir}{n}$	iuireni	I spent
	aha-u-$\frac{*}{*}$	ahau	period
	aa	aa	long
	m	em	of
	rnp-$\frac{t}{*}{w}$	renput	years
	$\frac{kh}{r}$	kher	under
	hem-$\frac{*}{n}$	hem-en	the majesty of
	nb	nebi	my Lord
	her	Her	the Horus
	wah-ankh	Wah-ankh	"Enduring of life"
	nisu-bit	Ensu-bit	"He of the reed and the bee"
CARTOUCHE	Sa-ra-in-$\frac{n}{t}{f}$	Sa-ra-intef	(THE PHARAOH) "Son of Ra : Intef"

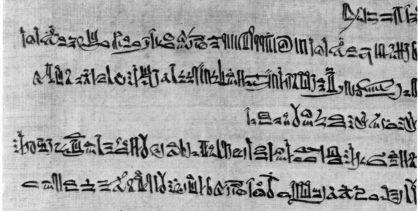

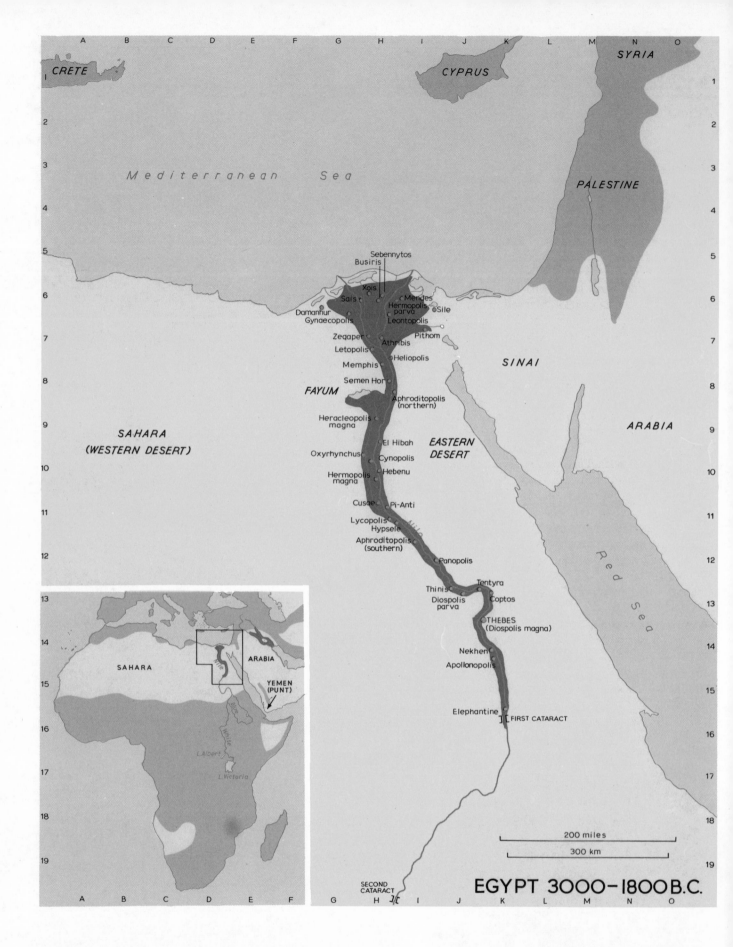

EGYPT 3000–1800 B.C.

CRETE

CYPRUS

SYRIA

PALESTINE

Mediterranean Sea

Sebennytos
Busiris
Xois
Mendes
Saïs
Hermopolis parva
Damanhur
Sile
Gynaecopolis
Leontopolis
Zeqaper
Pithom
Letopolis
Athribis
Memphis
Heliopolis
Semen Hor
FAYUM
Aphroditopolis (northern)
Heracleopolis magna
El Hibah
EASTERN DESERT
Oxyrhynchus
Cynopolis
Hermopolis magna
Hebenu
Cusae
Pi-Anti
Lycopolis
Hypsele
Aphroditopolis (southern)
Panopolis
Thinis
Tentyra
Diospolis parva
Coptos
THEBES (Diospolis magna)
Nekhen
Apollonopolis
Elephantine
FIRST CATARACT
SECOND CATARACT

SAHARA (WESTERN DESERT)

SINAI

ARABIA

Red Sea

Nile

200 miles
300 km

SAHARA

ARABIA

YEMEN (PUNT)

Blue
White
L.Albert
L.Victoria
Nile

The inset map of Africa shows how small a part of the Nile lies within Egypt. The White Nile rises in the Central African Highlands, the Blue Nile in Abyssinia, and after they have joined there is still Nubia to cross. Traditionally Egypt begins at the First Cataract (first when travelling upstream) below which the Nile is entirely navigable. The modern frontier is at the Second Cataract, 320 km to the south.

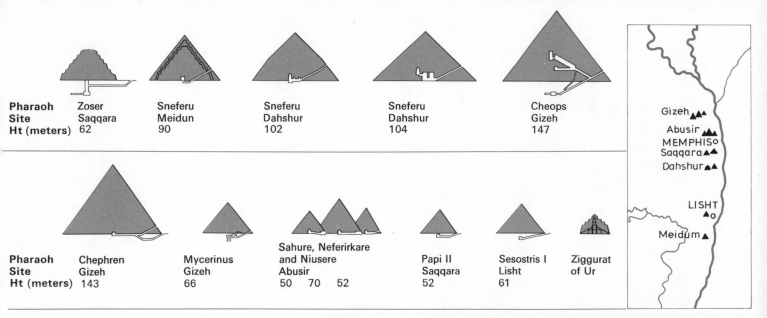

Pharaoh Site Ht (meters)	Zoser Saqqara 62	Sneferu Meidun 90	Sneferu Dahshur 102	Sneferu Dahshur 104	Cheops Gizeh 147

Pharaoh Site Ht (meters)	Chephren Gizeh 143	Mycerinus Gizeh 66	Sahure, Neferirkare and Niusere Abusir 50 70 52	Papi II Saqqara 52	Sesostris I Lisht 61	Ziggurat of Ur

THE PYRAMIDS

The Ancient Egyptian spent much of his life preparing for death and the kings of Egypt made their preparations on a monumental scale. Right from the start the pharaohs built sturdy tombs and furnished them with everything necessary to keep up their standard of living in the next world.

King Zoser, founder of the Third Dynasty, aimed to outdo all his predecessors. He not only did that but started something that became the outstanding characteristic of Ancient Egyptian society: pyramid building.

Zoser's building was not really a pyramid: it had a rectangular base, not a square one, and rose in a series of steps. These characteristics it shared with the Sumerian ziggurat and it may be that the idea – like the idea of writing – was imported from Mesopotamia. But Zoser's ziggurat was built of stone, not brick. It was built to mark a tomb, not carry a temple. And it was built to last. It still stands at Saqqara.

Zoser's successors started a number of step-pyramids on square bases. None of them was ever finished until Sneferu, first pharaoh of the Fourth Dynasty, completed one at Meidun. Sneferu did not stop at this point: he cased in the original step-pyramid to make a true pyramid. Then he built two more at Dahshur. One of the Dahshur pyramids has a change of angle halfway up but the other is a true pyramid, though its slope is low (43 degrees against the 52 degrees usual later). This is the first pyramid designed as such from the start.

The next three pharaohs built the three Great Pyramids of Gizeh. After that who could compete? Pyramids became smaller and were built with a rubble core which was cheaper but has lasted less well. None of the Fifth and Sixth Dynasty pyramids is in very good shape now.

Pyramid-building stopped during the First Intermediate Period. The Middle Kingdom

The Pyramids are all situated between the Delta and the Fayum on the edge of the Western Desert. They lie within a day's ride of Memphis (the Old Kingdom capital) or Lisht (the Middle Kingdom capital). The names of the different groups – Gizeh, Saqqara, etc – are modern.

18 The three Pyramids of Gizeh.

pharaohs of the Twelfth Dynasty, anxious to revive the splendors of the Old Kingdom, put up some fair-sized examples near their capital Lisht and at Saqqara. They had mud-brick cores and have crumbled badly.

With the end of the Middle Kingdom the Pyramid Age was over. A pyramid was a giant signpost to buried treasure and the tombs they held were quickly found and robbed.

21

19 Drawing of a carving on an Egyptian stone mace head. It dates from just before the unification of Egypt (3000 BC). The row of standards along the top is unfortunately far from complete but the central five can be identified as the totems of Upper Egyptian Nomes 12, 11, 9, 11 again, 17. The one on the right-hand fragment is an early form of the falcon god Anti of Upper Egyptian Nome 18.

The standards facing right carry captive lapwings – this represents the defeat of a lapwing clan that must have lived somewhere in the Delta. The standards facing left carry bows. Bows were used as a symbol for Nubians throughout Egyptian history; lapwings do not appear again.

In the main part of the picture a king is performing an agricultural ceremony among the irrigation canals. He is wearing the White Crown of Upper Egypt. His hieroglyphic sign (in front of his face) is a scorpion. This is either King Menes himself or an immediate predecessor.

Before Egypt was united, Egyptians thought of themselves in terms of their clan and its totem.

These totems were housed in temples, carried in procession on feast days and borne as standards in battle. They were usually figures of animals – a dog, a bull or a crocodile, for example. But some clans had fetishes (sacred objects) rather than totems in the strict sense: for example, a weapon such as a spear or a symbol of power such as a scepter.

With the unification of the country the totems of the strongest clans became the insignia of the provinces (called "nomes") and the gods of the Kingdom. Each acquired special attributes.

One of the Delta nomes, for instance, had as its totem the ibis bird: the Ibis-god Thoth became the god of wisdom and the patron saint of scribes throughout Egypt. He had shrines in many nomes besides his own.

This point is important: it could mean that the main temple in the capital of a nome might be dedicated to a god quite different from the official deity of the nome.

Egyptian hieroglyphic writing is difficult to decipher and many readings remain uncertain. For this reason the towns of ancient Egypt are always referred to by their Greek names. These are sometimes simply Greek spellings of the Egyptian name – for example, Memphis is the Greek form of Men-nefer – but sometimes they are Greek translations of the Egyptian animal or god.

For example, the capital of the nome of the Dog was called "Cynopolis" ("City of the Dog" in Greek). The Ibis-god Thoth was equated by the Greeks with their god Hermes so the capital of the nome of the Ibis was called Hermopolis.

As explained above, the nome capital might well have a different god from that of the nome as a whole: the capital of the Hare nome worshipped the Ibis-god Thoth and so became another Hermopolis in Greek. In this case the two Hermopoli are distinguished as "great" and "little" (magna and parva), but in many cases no distinction was made. As there could be as many as six towns with the same Greek name it is often difficult to know which one is meant.

20 Mycerinus, builder of the Third Pyramid, between two female figures – on the left the goddess Hathor, on the right a goddess symbolising Nome 17 of Upper Egypt.

A whole series of these triple groups was found in the funeral temple of Mycerinus' pyramid, the only difference between them being in the right-hand figure which bears a different nome totem in each.

Ancient Egyptian names are in capitals, modern Arabic names in italics

THE NOMES OF LOWER EGYPT

Conventional number	Hieroglyph	Name	Nome Capital
1		The White Wall	Memphis
2		The Thigh	Letopolis, the town goddess, being equated with Leto, mother of Apollo
3		The West	Gynaecopolis (city of the female), the town goddess being the cow HATHOR
4		The Crossed Arrows (Upper Province)	ZEQAPER (*Kom Manous*), probably the Greek Prosopis
5		The Crossed Arrows (Lower Province)	Sais
6		The Mountain Bull	Xois
7		The Western Spear	*Damanhur*
8		The Eastern Spear	PITHOM
9		The God ANDJTI	Busiris
10		The Black Bull	Athribis
11		The HESEB Bull	Leontopolis (city of the lion) after the local lion god
12		The Cow and Calf	Sebennytos
13		The Sceptre of ANDJTI	Heliopolis (city of the sun) as the town god was the sun god HARAKHTE
14		The Eastern Store	Sile
15		The Ibis	Hermopolis parva, the Ibis god THOTH being equated with Hermes (cf. Upper Egyptian nome 15)
16		The Dolphin	Mendes

THE NOMES OF UPPER EGYPT

Conventional number	Hieroglyph	Name	Nome Capital
22		The Knife	Aphroditopolis, the town goddess being the cow HATHOR who was equated with Aphrodite
21		The Palm Tree (Lower Province)	SEMEN HOR
20		The Palm Tree (Upper Province)	Heracleopolis magna, the ram HERISHEF who was the town god being equated with Heracles
19		The Sceptre UAB	Oxyrhynchus ("sharp-nose"). This is the Greek name for a pike-like fish that was the town totem
18		The Falcon ANTI	Uncertain: perhaps at *El Hibah*
17		The Black Dog	Cynopolis (city of the dog)
16		The Oryx	HEBENU (*Kom el Ahmar*)
15		The Hare	Hermopolis magna, the town god THOTH being equated with Hermes (cf. Lower Egyptian nome 15)
14		The Tree and Viper (Lower Province)	Cusae
13		The Tree and Viper (Upper Province)	Lycopolis (city of the wolf), the town god being the wolf UPUANT
12		The Mountain and Viper	PI-ANTI (*Deir el Gebrawi*)
11		The SET animal	Hypsele
10		The Cobra	Aphroditopolis (southern; cf. Upper Egyptian nome 22)
9		The Fetish MIN	Panopolis. The fetish took the form of a phallus so the Greeks equated MIN with Pan
8		The Fetish TA-UR	Thinis
7		The Fetish BAT	Diospolis parva (cf. Upper Egyptian nome 4 and, on page 26, Lower Egyptian nome 17)
6		The Crocodile	Tentyra
5		The Two Falcons	Coptos
4		The Sceptre WASET	In the imperial period the capital was Thebes, also known as Diospolis magna because Amen, the god of Thebes, was identified with Zeus and Dios is the genitive of Zeus; hence "city of Zeus." The original capital was at Hermunthis, 13 miles upstream (19 km.)
3		The town NEKHEN	NEKHEN was the town of the falcon god HORUS, so the Greeks called it Hieraconpolis, "city of the falcon." By the imperial period the town on the opposite bank was more important. This was NEKHEB, the seat of the vulture goddess of the same name. The Greeks identified her with Eileithyia, their goddess of childbrith; hence Eileithyiapolis
2		The Falcon HORUS	Apollinopolis magna, HORUS being equated with Apollo
1		TA-SETET (The Land of Granite?)	Elephantine. Which suggests that the original totem may have been an elephant, but could merely be a reference to ivory trading at this frontier post

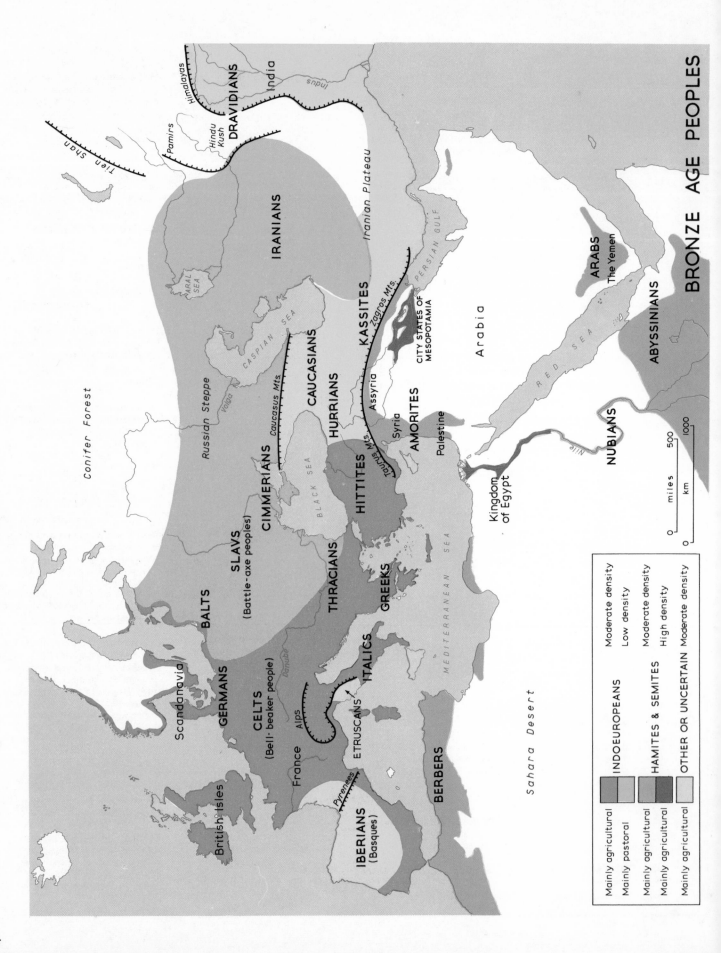

BRONZE AGE PEOPLES

DRAVIDIANS
India
Himalayas
Indus
Tien Shan
Pamirs
Hindu Kush
IRANIANS
Iranian Plateau
ARAL SEA
CASPIAN SEA
KASSITES
Zagros Mts.
PERSIAN GULF
ARABS
The Yemen
Russian Steppe
Volga
Caucasus Mts.
CAUCASIANS
HURRIANS
Assyria
CITY STATES OF MESOPOTAMIA
Arabia
ABYSSINIANS
Conifer Forest
BLACK SEA
CIMMERIANS
SLAVS
(Battle-axe peoples)
HITTITES
Taurus Mts.
Syria
AMORITES
Palestine
RED SEA
NUBIANS
Nile
Kingdom
of Egypt
BALTS
THRACIANS
GREEKS
MEDITERRANEAN SEA
Scandanavia
GERMANS
CELTS
(Bell-beaker people)
France
Alps
Danube
ITALICS
ETRUSCANS
Pyrenees
British Isles
IBERIANS
(Basques)
BERBERS
Sahara Desert

0   500
miles
0   1000
km

INDOEUROPEANS	Moderate density
	Low density
HAMITES & SEMITES	Moderate density
	High density
OTHER OR UNCERTAIN	Moderate density

Mainly agricultural
Mainly pastoral
Mainly agricultural
Mainly agricultural
Mainly agricultural

Europe and the Near East in the Bronze Age 1800 BC

In this map we are looking at two things: the different sorts of people who lived in Europe and the Near East and how many of them there were in each part.

The different peoples have already been introduced on page 12: the two main races are the Indo-Europeans across Europe and Russia, and the Hamites and Semites (Berbers and Arabs) of North Africa and Arabia. Besides these two there are the Dravidians in India (of which the map shows the far west – the Valley of the Indus), the Caucasians in the mountains north and east of Mesopotamia and some non-Indo-European peoples in Europe (the Etruscans in Italy and the Iberians in Spain).

The most widely spread of the western Indo-Europeans at this time were the people known to later history as the Celts. They had a characteristic drinking-vessel, which archaeologists call a "bell beaker" (because it is shaped like an upturned bell). As bell beakers have been found all over western Europe, from Spain and Britain to Germany, this can be taken as the range of Celts at the time. The far western part – Spain and Britain – had probably been fairly recently won from other peoples like the Iberians (the present-day Basques).

The Indo-Europeans of east Europe were more pastoral than those in the west, that is to say they put more effort into raising stock (cattle, sheep and goats) than into plowing and planting. As a result they were more inclined to wander and indeed, on the Russian steppe where the grazing is poor and the flocks have to be moved along all the time, they became true nomads shifting their tents every week. This mobile way of life carried the eastern Indo-Europeans deep into Asia, round the Caspian and Aral Seas and on to the Iranian Plateau.

At the same time other Indo-Europeans – the Hittites – moved from Europe across the Dardanelles into Anatolia. As a result, the Caucasians were gripped in an Indo-European pincer movement which was to squeeze them hard.

One of the contrasts between crop-growers and stock-breeders is their very different numbers on the land. Roughly speaking, a given piece of land will support ten times as many crop-growers as stock-breeders. This is because it yields much more food as crops than it does as milk or meat from grazing animals.

Actual figures for Bronze Age times can only be guessed at but they would range from 100 people per square kilometer in river valleys where irrigating agriculture took place, down to 4 per square kilometer for ordinary crop-growing country and only 4 per 10 square kilometers for stock-breeders. This means that Egypt (20,000 square kilometers of irrigating agriculture), France (500,000 square kilometers of ordinary agriculture) and European Russia (5,000,000 square kilometers, mostly grazing country or forest at this time) all had much the same population – about 2 million.

At first sight one might think that the stock-breeders could hardly attack the more numerous crop-growers with much hope of success. But they could (and did) for two reasons. In the first place, the more densely settled areas were the first to be unified politically – and when internal fighting stopped the arts of war declined. By contrast, the wandering tribes of the steppe were constantly quarrelling over grazing rights which kept them in fighting trim all the time.

The other factor is that mobility is the key to successful warfare and mobility is the nomads' way of life. Although in this era no one was riding horses to battle, the east Indo-European peoples had tamed horses well enough to make them pull chariots. And with these chariots they could scatter much larger armies of peasant infantry. Thanks to this decisive weapon the Indo-Europeans in the Near East were to have an impact out of all proportion to their numbers.

The story is a complicated one. Roughly a hundred years or so after the date of this map:

1. East Iranians (Aryans) descended on the Dravidians of the Indus Valley, massacred them and moved on to occupy the rest of north India.
2. West Iranians, pushing the Kassites of the Zagros ahead of them, overran Mesopotamia and founded a new dynasty that ruled Babylonia (the old Sumer and Akkad) for the next 400 years.
3. Perhaps because the Hittites were attacking them the Caucasian Hurrians descended on Syria and Assyria. Eventually an Iranian clan called the Mitanni created a kingdom embracing both these countries.
4. Lower Egypt (the Delta) was overrun by mysterious invaders whom the Egyptians called the "Hyksos." The majority of the Hyksos were probably Amorite Bedouin from the Arabian desert but as they owed their success to chariots (which the Egyptians had never seen before) they were probably led by Indo-Europeans.

The Egyptian Empire 1400 BC

22 Rameses II in his war chariot.

The Hyksos invaders ruled Egypt for about 150 years. Their capital was at Tanis in the east corner of the Delta. A native Egyptian dynasty (at Thebes) ruled the most southerly fourteen nomes as vassals of the Hyksos.[1]

About 1550 BC one of the princes of Thebes rebelled against the Hyksos, beat them and took and destroyed Tanis. Egypt was liberated and the most glorious phase in its history – known either as "the New Kingdom" or "the Empire" – began.

"The Empire" is the better name: the warrior pharaohs of the Eighteenth Dynasty conquered and ruled territories outside the natural boundaries of Egypt. They advanced in two directions: through Palestine to Syria and up the Nile into Nubia. Amosis, founder of the dynasty, invaded Palestine and his son Amenophis I conquered Nubia as far as the Second Cataract.

Then came the two most formidable pharaohs Egypt ever had: Tutmosis I and, soon after, Tutmosis III. Tutmosis I conquered Palestine and Syria and advanced up the Nile to the Third Cataract. Tutmosis III actually campaigned on the far side of the Euphrates as well as reaching the Fourth Cataract in the Nile Valley. These were the limits of Egyptian advance. Indeed, in Syria the frontier was soon pushed back by the Mitanni (pp. 25, 30). In the end the two powers agreed on a division of the country which left only the southern half to Egypt. This is the state of the Empire shown on the map opposite.

Amenophis IV, who ruled the Empire in the 1350s, was no soldier but he is still one of the most famous of the Eighteenth Dynasty pharaohs. He tried to get rid of the clutter of animal-headed gods and local fetishes and establish something nearer to our idea of religion.

He believed in only one god, the sun god Aten. He changed his name from Amenophis (meaning "Amen is satisfied") to Akhenaten ("pleasing to Aten"). And, to get away from the many temples of Amen at Thebes, he built a new capital in the Hare nome called Akhetaten ("the horizon of Aten"). The Egyptian peasants must have understood very little of his ideas, the priests certainly hated him. Soon after his death the new religion was overthrown, its inscriptions erased and the old order restored.

While Akhanaten was busy with his religious reforms the Hittites destroyed the kingdom of the Mitanni, took over northern Syria and began to press south. Once again it was a time for warrior pharaohs and army commanders soon ousted the feeble descendants of Akhenaten. One of these generals, Rameses I, founded the Nineteenth Dynasty which fought hard and often against the Hittites.

The period was a prosperous one with much building: Rameses II in particular built an enormous number of temples up and down the country, including the rock-cut monster shrine at Abu Simbel in Nubia. They were dedicated to himself as much as to the gods and were covered with reliefs of his "victories." In fact his famous "victory" at Kadesh over the Hittites was really a defeat while his triumphs over the Nubians were entirely imaginary (Nubia had already been pacified). Nevertheless, it was partly thanks to Rameses that the Hittites were brought to a halt at the frontier of Palestine and that Egypt kept this province for another 100 years.[2]

The Palestinians themselves caused Egypt no trouble: they were too divided. Each of the villages shown on the map had a king of its own who spent most of his time complaining to the Egyptian Governor about his neighbors.

Under the Empire four new nomes were created in the eastern Delta which suggests that population there was increasing.[3] The four are:

Conventional number	Hieroglyph	Name	Nome Capital
17		The Throne (the hieroglyphs are phonetic, not pictorial)	Diospolis parva (c.f. Upper Egyptian nomes 4 and 7)
18		The Prince (Upper Province)	Bubastis
19		The Prince (Lower Province)	IMET
20		The East	Saft el Hennah

Nome 19 lay around the Hyksos capital Tanis, destroyed during the war of liberation. Tanis was rebuilt by Rameses II who called it Pi-Rameses ("City of Rameses"): it quickly became more important than Imet, the official nome capital. For the rebuilding of Tanis, Rameses used slave labor, in particular captured Hebrews. At this time Hebrew was a word used for the nomads living in and around Palestine and Syria.

The Hebrews laboring at Pi-Rameses and at near-by Pithom, the capital of Nome 8, managed to overpower their guards and flee in a body to Sinai. There they became the nucleus of the Israeli nation which moved into Palestine in the confused period about 1200 BC. Three thousand years later the quarrel is still going on, which is a long time even for the Near East.

[1] The Hyksos make up the Fifteenth and Sixteenth Dynasties and the vassal princes of Thebes are the Seventeenth.

[2] It was known as Canaan at this time: the word "Palestine" is a variant of "Philistine" and only came into use in the Iron Age (see p. 34).

[3] The population of the Empire was probably about 3 million of whom 250,000 would have been Palestinians and 100,000 Nubians.

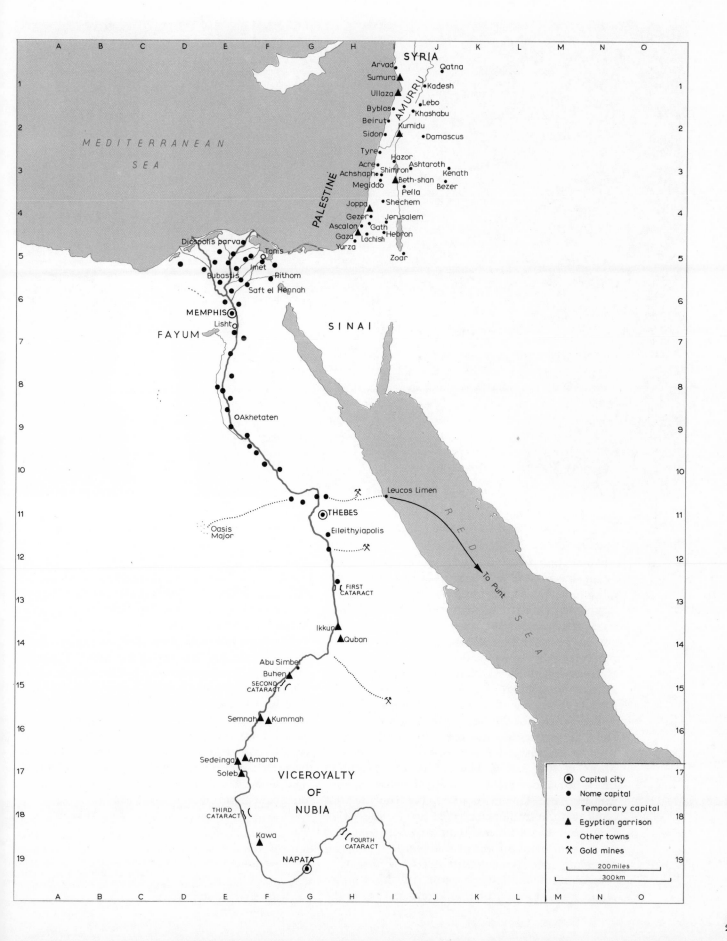

SYRIA

Arvad •
Sumura ▲   • Qatna
Ullaza ▲   • Kadesh
Byblos •   • Lebo
Beirut •   • Khashabu
Sidon •   ▲ Kumidu
Tyre •   • Damascus
Acre •   Hazor
Achshaph • Shimron ▲ Ashtaroth
Megiddo •   Beth-shan ▲ • Kenath
                 • Bezer
             • Pella
Joppa ▲   • Shechem
Gezer •
Ascalon • • Jerusalem
Gaza ▲ Gath •
Lachish • • Hebron
Yurza •
     Zoar •

AMURRU

PALESTINE

MEDITERRANEAN
SEA

Diospolis parva •
     ○ Tanis
Bubastis • Imet
     • Rithom
Saft el Hennah •

MEMPHIS ◉
    ○ Lisht

FAYUM

SINAI

○ Akhetaten

Oasis
Major ○

Leucos Limen •

⊙ THEBES

Eileithyiapolis •

FIRST
CATARACT

Ikkur •
     ▲ Quban

Abu Simbel •
Buhen ▲
SECOND
CATARACT

Semnah ▲ ▲ Kummah

Sedeinga ▲ ▲ Amarah
Soleb ▲

VICEROYALTY
OF
NUBIA

THIRD
CATARACT

Kawa ▲

NAPATA ◉

FOURTH
CATARACT

RED SEA

To Punt

◉	Capital city
●	Nome capital
○	Temporary capital
▲	Egyptian garrison
•	Other towns
⚒	Gold mines

200 miles
300 km

Thebes of the 100 Gates

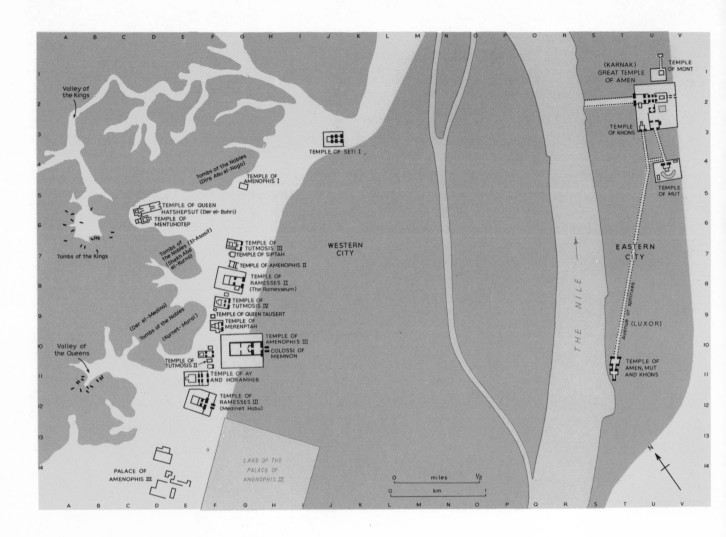

Thebes, the capital of the Egyptian Empire, lay either side of the Nile. The mud-brick houses of the inhabitants have long since disappeared but in the rainless climate the stone monuments have survived thirty centuries of neglect. On the east bank are the giant temples of the gods, on the west the funeral temples of the pharaohs.

Temples and shrines had been built at Thebes since at least Middle Kingdom times. During the Empire they were all rebuilt on a colossal scale.

The greatest of the builders was Amenophis III. He was responsible for the core of the Great Temple of Amen, for the subsidiary temples of Mont, of Mut and of Amen, Mut and Khons to the south and for the avenues of sphinxes connecting them. He also built a palace on the west bank, with an ornamental lake two miles long in front of it and a funeral temple (where he could be prayed for). In front of this temple stood two 20-meter, 1000-tonne granite statues of himself.[1]

Like all the other pharaohs of the Empire Amenophis III was buried, in a tomb cut out of the rock in what is called "the Valley of the Kings." Rock tombs replaced pyramids because all the Old Kingdom pyramids had already been robbed and it was thought an obscure tomb would stand a better chance against thieves.

In fact, all the tombs in the Valley of the Kings were found and robbed too – except for one. Suitably, this belonged to the most obscure of all the Eighteenth Dynasty pharaohs, Tutenkhamen. The intact tomb of this short-lived son-in-law of Akhenaten was discovered by the English archaeologist Howard Carter in 1922. The innermost solid gold sarcophagus and the other treasures from the burial chambers are now in the Cairo Museum. The body was replaced in the outer stone sarcophagus which remains in the tomb.

[1] These are the statues the Greeks called "the Colossi of Memnon." Legend said the northern one made a ringing noise when the morning sun shone on it. Perhaps cracking noises did come from the statue as it heated up – it was already broken by then. It certainly never sounded again after the Roman Emperor Septimius Severus had it repaired.

23 Gold coffin of Tutankhamen. The young Pharaoh was buried in a nest of three coffins – stone, gilded wood and solid gold. This is the innermost, 22-carat gold 1 inch thick. ▶

24 Approach to the Temple of Amen, Mut and Khons at Luxor (map T10) showing the avenue of sphinxes laid out by Amenophis III and the outer pylon built by Rameses II.

Note the four grooves in the sloping faces of the pylons: these were for flagpoles. Rameses II put two obelisks and six colossal statues of himself in front of the temple. Three of the statues and one of the obelisks are still there. The other obelisk was moved to the Place de la Concorde in Paris in 1836.

25 Funerary temple of Queen Hatshepsut (map D5), the only queen to rule the Egyptian Empire. Hatshepsut chose an unusual design for a funerary temple. It was based on, and built next to, the temple of a Middle Kingdom pharaoh, Mentuhotep. It consisted of two terraces with a courtyard (now vanished) on top, and a sanctuary cut into the cliff behind. The simple architecture makes a fine contrast to the rugged cliffs.

26 The Temple of Horus at Apollonopolis magna, capital of Upper Egyptian Nome 2.

This is the best-preserved temple in Egypt; it was built a thousand years after the Theban temples – to be exact in 237–212 BC. However, the style is just the same. At the front (the far end) are massive pylons flanking the entrance. Then there is an open court with a colonnade round it. Then comes a high, pillared hall and, finally, the sanctuary which contained the image of the god.

In the case of more important temples extra pylons and courts were added on. The most important of all – the Great Temple of Amen at Karnak – finally had five pairs of pylons on the main axis and four more pairs on the side approach from the Temple of Mut (map U2).

Pylon is the Greek for "gate." You can see why the Greeks called the Egyptian capital "Thebes of the 100 Gates."

Power Politics 1400 – 1300 BC

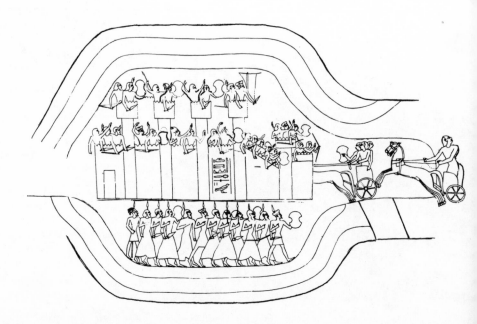

27 Hittite soldier.

The arc of arable land from Palestine, through Syria, to Mesopotamia is called "the Fertile Crescent."

The two areas of irrigating agriculture, Egypt and Babylonia, can be regarded as expansions at either end of the arc. They were the traditional powers of the region. In 1400 the Egyptians controlled Palestine and south Syria but the Babylonians, who had often extended north in the past, were in a quiet phase and ruled only their own part of Mesopotamia.

The middle of the Fertile Crescent (north Syria and north Mesopotamia) was in the hands of the Iranian Mitanni who had conquered it in the preceding century (p. 25). The Mitanni formed a bridge between the two traditional powers and put an end to their isolation. By 1400 these three powers had settled down peacefully together. Their kings corresponded with each other about frontier disputes and matters of trade. They made formal treaties and sealed them by exchanging princesses in marriage.

This tranquil state of affairs was shattered by the Hittites.

From their capital at Hattusas in the bend of the Halys River, the Hittite kings ruled over the Anatolian plateau. They constantly tried to impose their authority on the peoples around them – the Caucasians on their east frontier, the Cilicians (vassals of the Mitanni) to the south and the Arzawans to the east.

When the Hittites were successful in their local wars they looked farther afield, in particular at the rich provinces of the Fertile Crescent. They made a brief series of attacks about 1600 BC and a more sustained series about 1370 BC. The second was a disaster for the Mitanni, whose empire was destroyed, and a shock for the Egyptians who found themselves bundled back to Palestine. A son of the Hittite King moved into Carchemish as Viceroy of Syria.

On the collapse of the Mitanni the Assyrians regained their freedom. They quickly built up their state and became one of the four powers among whom the Fertile Crescent was now divided. Assyrian kings proved to be aggressive, always attacking their neighbors. This policy was not very successful in Bronze Age times but was to bring spectacular results in the Iron Age (p. 36).

The first certain event in European history comes in this period: the conquest of the Minoan kingdom of Crete by the Greeks.[1] Crete and the other Aegean islands have been Greek ever since. Greeks were probably getting a grip on Cyprus at the same time but we really know very little about this first phase of Greek history. A century later, thanks to Homer, we know a great deal more.

[1] "Minoan" is a word used by archaeologists: we do not know what these first Cretans called themselves.

28 Hittite charioteers fleeing into the town of Kadesh after being defeated by the Egyptians.

This representation of what was really an Egyptian defeat was carved by Rameses II on the outer pylons of both the Temple of Amen, Mut and Khons at Luxor (map 28 T11) and his funeral temple, the Ramasseum (G8). Note the moat round Kadesh, the archers on its walls and fresh Hittite troops moving out towards the battlefield.

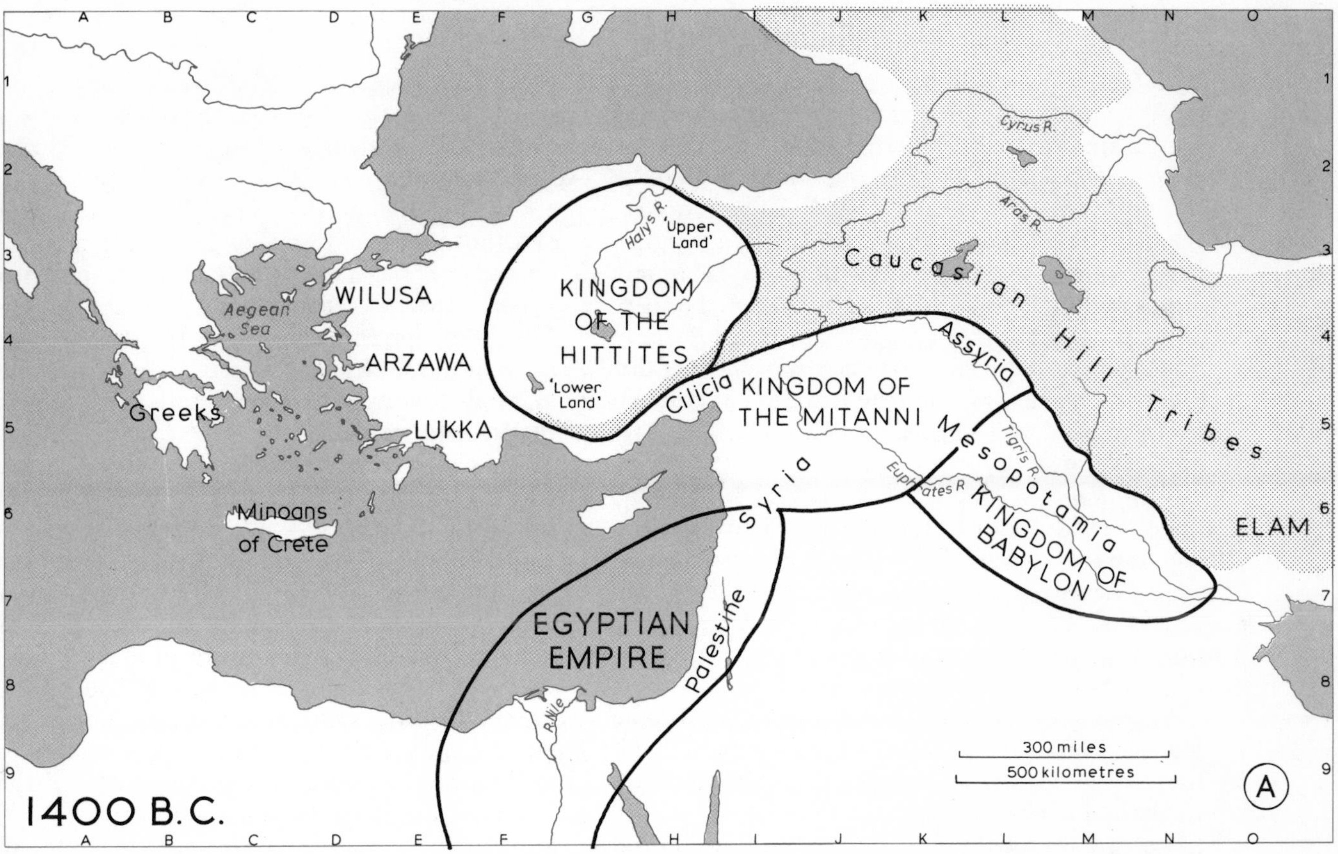
1400 B.C.
A
Greeks
Minoans of Crete
Aegean Sea
WILUSA
ARZAWA
LUKKA
KINGDOM OF THE HITTITES
Halys R.
'Upper Land'
'Lower Land'
Cilicia
KINGDOM OF THE MITANNI
Syria
Palestine
EGYPTIAN EMPIRE
R. Nile
Assyria
Mesopotamia
Euphrates R.
Tigris R.
KINGDOM OF BABYLON
Caucasian Hill Tribes
Cyrus R.
Aras R.
ELAM
300 miles
500 kilometres

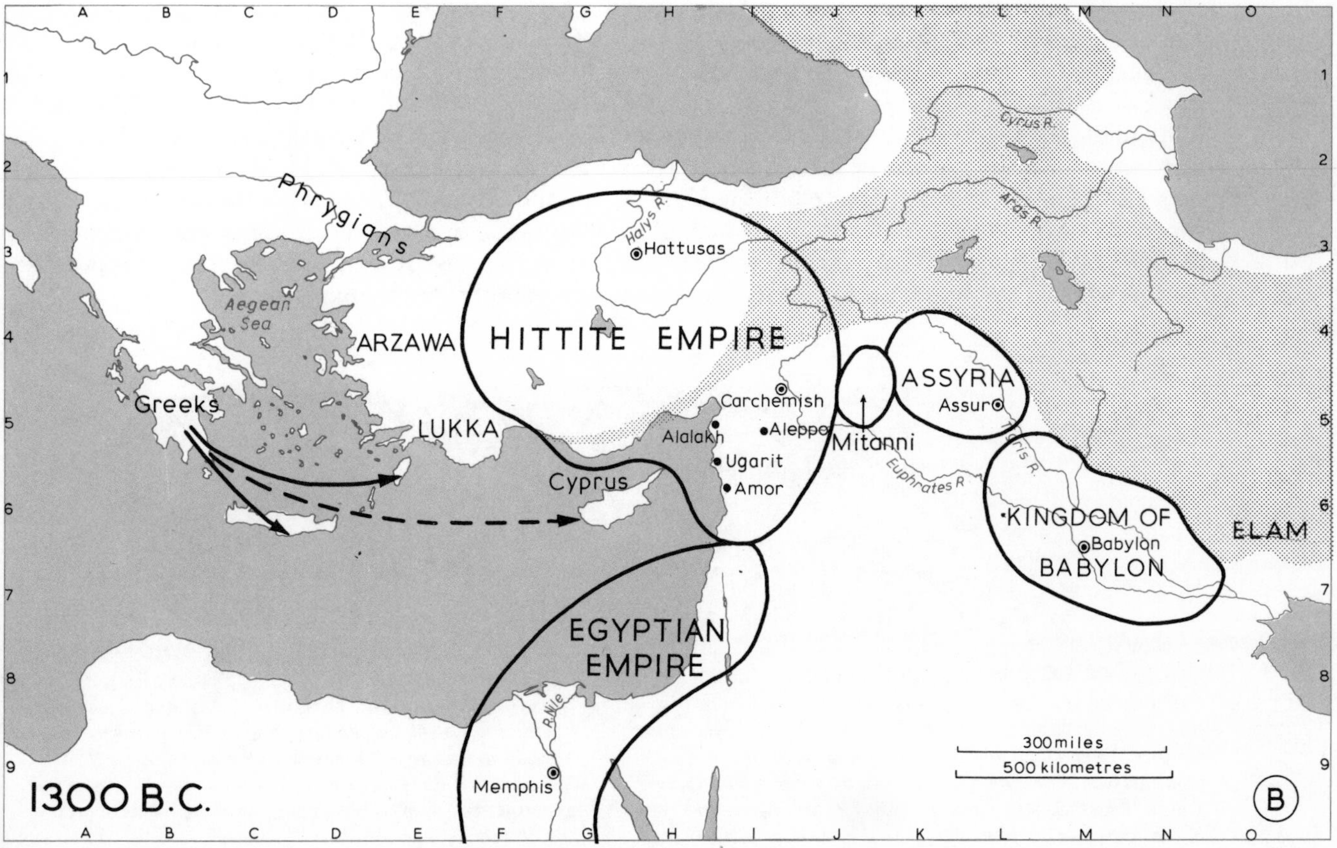
1300 B.C.
B
Phrygians
Greeks
Aegean Sea
ARZAWA
LUKKA
Cyprus
HITTITE EMPIRE
Halys R.
Hattusas
Carchemish
Alalakh
Aleppo
Ugarit
Amor
Mitanni
ASSYRIA
Assur
Euphrates R.
Tigris R.
KINGDOM OF BABYLON
Babylon
ELAM
Cyrus R.
Aras R.
EGYPTIAN EMPIRE
R. Nile
Memphis
300 miles
500 kilometres

Bronze Age Greece and the War with Troy
1250 BC

29 Mycenaean soldier.

The Greek peninsula is a mountain range that slants down into the sea as it runs south. Between the mountains are a few fertile valleys which have been focal points all through the history of Greece.

The farthest north and biggest is Macedonia, the next is Thessaly. South of this is a narrow valley known in Bronze Age times as Pelasgian Argos and later on as Malis. Then, after the strip of coast called Locris, comes the plain of Boeotia (pronounced Bee-o-sha). Attica is the elbow of the peninsula. A narrow arm (the Isthmus of Corinth) leads to the four-fingered hand in which the peninsula ends.

This hand is the Peloponnesus. The stubby finger next to Attica, and the web between this and the long second finger is the Argolis: in the web is an Argos more important than the one in the north. The web between the second and third fingers is Lacedaemon with its capital of Sparta. The fourth finger is Messene.

Besides the mainland the Bronze Age Greeks (or Achaeans, as they called themselves) also held the Ionian islands at the mouth of the Gulf of Corinth, Euboea on the coast and, to the south, the biggest of all the Greek islands, Crete. From Crete they were at this time island-hopping up towards the Anatolian coast using Carpathos, Rhodes and Cos as stepping-stones.

The most impressive ruins of the period are those of the Castle of Mycenae (F9): its walls are built of stones so big that later Greeks thought they must have been hewn by giants. There were many kings in Bronze Age Greece but the kings of Mycenae – a dynasty that legend said had been founded by Perseus – were recognized as overlords by the whole Peloponnesus. And after Atreus of

Mycenae captured and destroyed Thebes, the capital of Boeotia, Mycenaean suzerainty was extended over both Boeotia and Thessaly. It was Atreus' son and heir Agamemnon who, about 1250 BC, led the united forces of the Achaeans across the Aegean to besiege Troy. The sack of Troy (after a siege that was said to have lasted ten years) was the Achaean high-water mark.

The map opposite shows the situation in the Aegean at the time of the Trojan War. It is based on the roll call given by Homer in his epic account of the struggle, the *Iliad*.

As well as having a general authority over all Greece Agamemnon held Achaea and the Isthmus as his personal kingdom – a good central position for the overlord of the peninsula. The other pink areas are the subsidiary kingdoms, except that Thessaly, Boeotia and Elis had half a dozen kings each. The Ionian islanders were probably ruled by a single king but because one of their local lords, the cunning Odysseus of Ithaca, played an important part in the war and the poet wanted to make him more important than he really was the roll call becomes very muddled at this point.

Several of the names given here (the ones in brackets on the map) are not used by Homer. For example, he never refers to Messene as anything but the kingdom of Pylos. In some instances these names came into use at a later period, in other cases the omission may be just chance. Macedonia, however, is not mentioned under this or any other name. This is surprising: Macedonia at the time of the Trojan War was the home of the Dorian Greeks and it was the Dorians who, a generation after this, swept down on the Achaean kingdoms and obliterated them.

30 Linear B tablet. Writing spread to Europe in the second millennium BC. The scripts used were derived from the traditional syllabic scripts of the Near East but were much simpler. Each sign stood for a consonant-vowel combination. For example, the Greek script known as Linear B has signs for ma, me, mi, mo and mu – and that is the complete list of m signs. As there are 20 consonants and 5 vowels this sort of "open" syllabary ("open" because the syllables are never closed by a consonant) need only have 20×5=100 signs. The earlier syllabaries such as the Sumerian had several thousand signs.

Like all the other Linear B tablets known this is an account. It records the amount of olive oil delivered to the Palace of Mycenae.

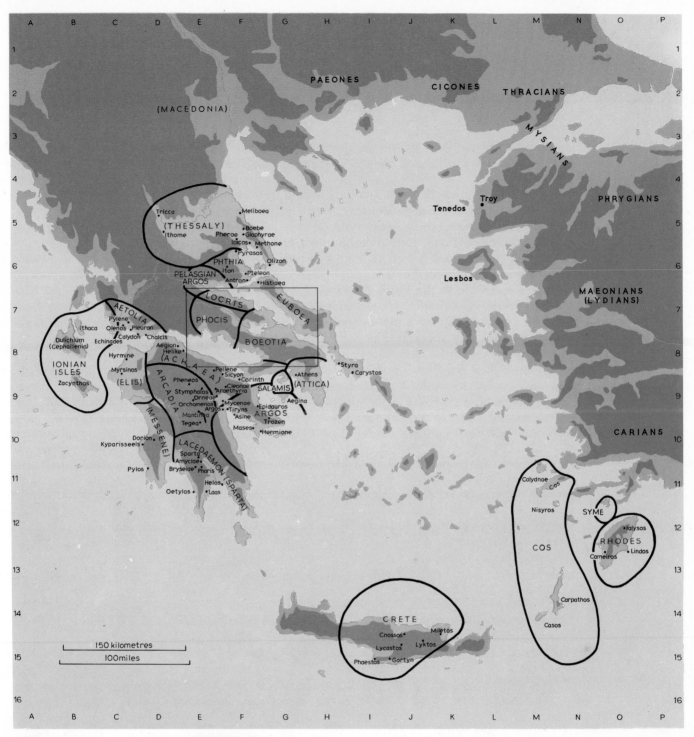

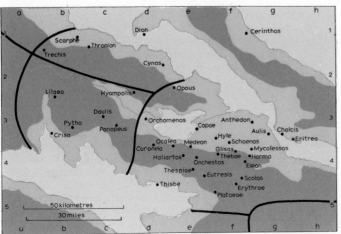

THE AEGEAN 1200 BC
The Greek States that fought against Troy are colored pink. Locris, Phocis and Boeotia are shown on an enlarged scale on the left. Land over 1000 feet is colored brown (mauve in the Achaean area). The lake in the middle of Boeotia, Lake Copais, was drained in the nineteenth century.

33

Iron beats Bronze 1200 – 1000 BC

31 Philistine soldier.

The Bronze Age came to an end in upheaval as barbarian warriors with iron swords overthrew the old empires.

Iron had been made in small amounts by the Hittites for several centuries before this. But they had not really mastered the process and their iron was very expensive. It cost forty times as much as silver – only kings could afford to buy a sword made of so expensive a metal.

Then, somewhere in the north Aegean region someone developed a simple way of making iron. Suddenly, from being far more expensive than bronze, iron became cheaper. The peoples with this valuable knowledge got themselves better swords than their neighbors, and they soon put their new swords to work. The Achaean Greek and Hittite empires crumbled before the attackers who swept on over Syria and Palestine. They were held – but only just – on the borders of Egypt and Assyria.

In Greece we know that the invaders were

people the Bible calls Philistines. Back in the Aegean the west Anatolian coast was settled by other Greeks (the Aeolians and Ionians) trying to escape from the troubles the Dorians had brought to their homeland.[1]

As a result of all this the Iron Age map looks very different from that of the Bronze Age. In Anatolia the Phrygians rule in place of the Hittites. In Syria the towns are now held by princes of Lydian or Lycian blood (historians call them neo-Hittites because their language is very like Hittite). However, in the confusion a good many Syrian towns have fallen into the hands of the Aramaean Bedouin.

Similarly, in Palestine the arrival of the Philistines on the coast has given the Israelites the chance to move in from the desert and seize a good part of the "Promised Land." The old empires are very much in eclipse. Egypt is confined to the Nile Valley and Babylonia has been overrun by another group of Aramaean tribes, the Chaldaeans.

[1] These Ionians have nothing to do with the Ionian islands on the far side of Greece. The name comes from the Athenians who used it to describe themselves and the Aegean islanders who spoke the same Greek dialect. Athens was one of the few states to hold out against the Dorians. She provided the leadership and much of the manpower for the migration that created Ionia.

The Aeolians came from Thessaly.

Dorian Greeks from Macedonia. In Anatolia they were the Phrygians and other peoples of the west – Lydians, Carians and Lycians. The Dorian movement petered out within the Aegean: Crete, Cos and Rhodes were their last conquests.

The refugee Achaeans (now only too aware of the advantages of iron) went a lot further. One group overran Cyprus and conquered parts of the south coast of Anatolia (Pamphylia and Cilicia). Another joined the conquerors of the Hittite Empire in the sack of Syria. From there they mounted an attack on Egypt and, although this was beaten back by the pharaoh Rameses III, they retreated only as far as Palestine. They are the

32 Rameses III, with the vulture goddess Mut hovering over his head, defeats the Philistines.

From left to right the boats are Egyptian – Philistine – Philistine. In the lowest row one Philistine boat has capsized and the other has been captured. Along the bottom of the picture Egyptian soldiers lead away captured Philistines whose arms have been tied together.

The Philistines were not a single people but a federation of tribes. Two of their boats have crews wearing horned helmets – where they came from is not known; it could be anywhere between the Aegean and the Levant. The other four, manned by soldiers with feather headdresses, are probably from Crete. A man wearing this sort of headdress figures in a Cretan inscription of the period.

The drawing is a copy of a relief in Rameses III's funerary temple at Medinet Habu, Thebes (map 28 F12).

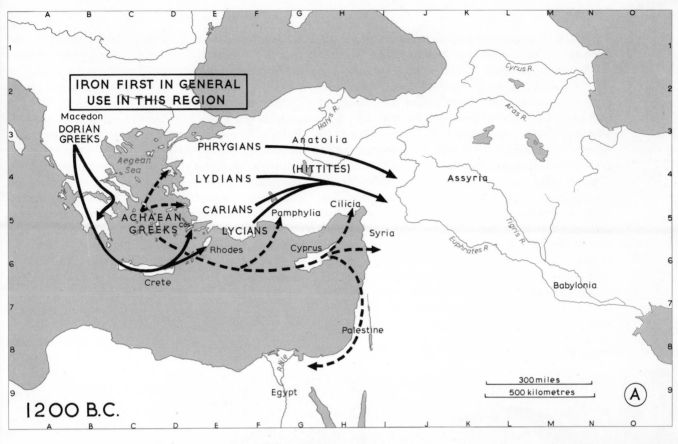

IRON FIRST IN GENERAL
USE IN THIS REGION

Macedon
DORIAN
GREEKS

*Aegean
Sea*

PHRYGIANS — Anatolia

LYDIANS (HITTITES)

CARIANS — Pamphylia — Cilicia

ACHAEAN
GREEKS — Cos.

LYCIANS — Cyprus — Syria

Rhodes

Crete

Palestine

Egypt

Halys R.

Assyria

Cyrus R.

Aras R.

Tigris R.

Euphrates R.

Babylonia

300 miles
500 kilometres

Ⓐ

1200 B.C.

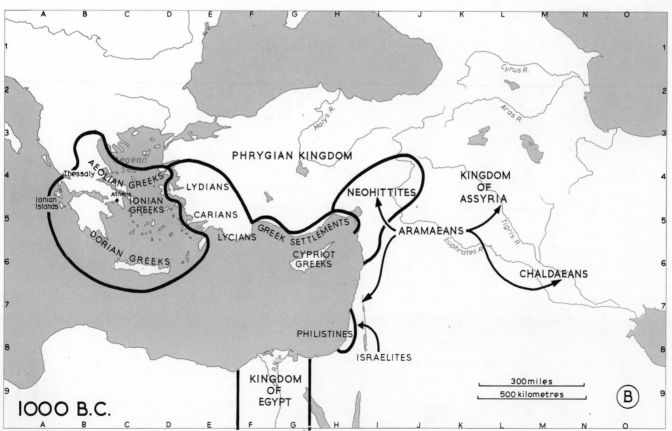

Halys R.

PHRYGIAN KINGDOM

Cyrus R.

Aras R.

Thessaly

AEOLIAN
GREEKS

Ionian
Islands

Athens

IONIAN
GREEKS

LYDIANS

CARIANS

KINGDOM
OF
ASSYRIA

NEOHITTITES

DORIAN
GREEKS

LYCIANS

GREEK SETTLEMENTS

ARAMAEANS

Tigris R.

Euphrates R.

CYPRIOT
GREEKS

CHALDAEANS

PHILISTINES

ISRAELITES

KINGDOM
OF
EGYPT

300 miles
500 kilometres

Ⓑ

1000 B.C.

The Rise and Fall of Assyria 900 – 612 BC

33 Assyrian soldier.

Assyria was well placed to dominate the Fertile Crescent, either by force or by trade.

The basis of trade in the region was the exchange of metals mined by the mountain peoples of the north for textiles and other manufactures produced by Mesopotamian craftsmen. Assyrians were the obvious middlemen for this traffic and in Bronze Age times we know Anatolia's copper exports were in the hands of Assyrian merchants. Undoubtedly Assyria drew a profit from trade throughout her history. However, in the Iron Age Assyria became a state dedicated to the arts of war; the figure of the merchant was replaced by that of the all-conquering king.

The advance of the Assyrian frontier was won by four kings in particular – Shalmaneser III, Tiglath Pilesar III, Esarhaddon and Assurbanipal – but all Assyrian kings fought hard and often. Only by continual fighting could they intimidate the frontier tribes and repress the frequent revolts within the Empire.

The Empire was really an incredible achievement. Assyria can have had no more than a quarter of a million inhabitants (about the same as Palestine) yet she conquered and held Babylonia and Syria (each of which would have had twice as many), Palestine and the whole mountain zone north and east of the Fertile Crescent. Finally she conquered Egypt which had twice as many inhabitants as the whole Fertile Crescent.[1]

But each time an old enemy was overthrown a new one appeared beyond. This was particularly true in the north where their victories carried the Assyrians farther and farther into the Taurus, the Armenian mountains and the Zagros.

Since the time of Tiglath Pilesar III (745–728)

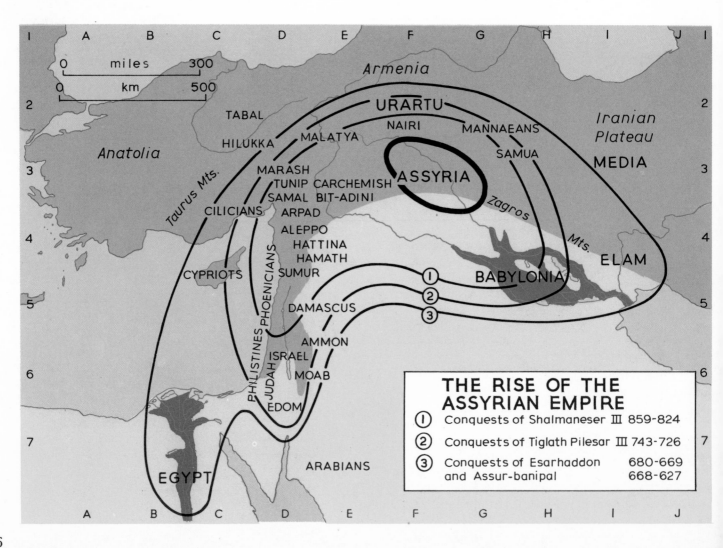

THE RISE OF THE ASSYRIAN EMPIRE

① Conquests of Shalmaneser III 859-824

② Conquests of Tiglath Pilesar III 743-726

③ Conquests of Esarhaddon 680-669 and Assur-banipal 668-627

The traditional capital of Assyria was Assur. In the ninth century a new, grander capital was built at Calah. There was another move during the reign of Sargon II (722–705) but Dur Shurrakin ("Fort Sargon") was abandoned at his death. In its place his son Sennacherib (705–681) built Nineveh, which remained the capital to the end of the Empire.

The area of Assur – less than 60 hectares – was about average for a Mesopotamian city. Calah covered 260 hectares and Nineveh over 750 hectares. This makes the later Assyrian capitals much the biggest cities the world had seen till then: Nineveh may well have held 100,000 people.

34 The Assyrian King Esarhaddon with the Egyptian Pharaoh and a king of the Phoenicians kneeling before him. The lips of the defeated monarchs are tied with thongs which Esarhaddon holds (together with his mace) in his left hand. We know that Esarhaddon never captured the Pharaoh – the thongs are symbolic, representing Assyrian control of Egypt. This was real enough, as was the Assyrians' capacity for cruelty. Thongs through the lips would have been a light punishment by their standards.

the Assyrians had been fighting the Medes of the Iranian plateau. Repeated defeats encouraged the Medes to unite. At this point the Assyrians found themselves fighting one power too many and, when the Medes went over to the offensive, Assyria suddenly collapsed. Assur was taken only a dozen years after Assurbanipal's death; two years after that a combined Median–Babylonian army sacked Calah and Nineveh. The cities were never occupied again: as a state Assyria ceased to exist.

herited David's capital, Jerusalem: Israel's kings moved from Schechem to Tirzah before finally settling in Samaria.

¹ In the late prehistoric phase (about 4000 BC) Egypt and Mesopotamia probably both had about a quarter of a million inhabitants. Egypt, with its salt problems confined to the fringe of the Delta, steadily expanded its agriculture and must have more than doubled its population every thousand years up to 1000 BC. Mesopotamia grew much more slowly: although it expanded in Assyria and Akkad this was partly balanced by the abandoning of the land in Sumer that had become too salty to cultivate.

THE HEBREWS IN PALESTINE 1200–725 BC

Between 1200 and 900 BC the Hebrews gradually conquered most of Palestine.

In its early days the nation consisted of twelve independent tribes who only cooperated when they had to. Just before 1000 BC, Philistine attacks became so dangerous that the tribes agreed to elect one king to lead them. This was Saul of Benjamin. Under his successor, David of Judah (990–968) the new kingdom defeated all its enemies and made them pay tribute.

David's reign was the high point for the Hebrew state and things continued to go well under his son Solomon (968–928). Then the Hebrews split up again: into the two kingdoms of Israel and Judah. Naturally the surrounding states – Damascus, Ammon, Moab, Edom and the five cities of the Philistines – reclaimed their independence. Squabbles between them and the Hebrew kingdoms (and between Judah and Israel themselves) went on all through the next 250 years. Finally (about 725) all these little fish were swallowed up by the Assyrians.

Traditionally ten tribes are ascribed to Israel and only two to Judah. In fact the division was more like eight to three because Benjamin as well as Simeon went with Judah, and Reuben's territory was conquered by Moab.

The administrative districts shown on the map are those of Solomon's time. Of the fourteen provinces, twelve are tribal areas (Zebulun is counted in with Asher but Gad is divided in two) and two are coastal areas conquered by David. Judah in-

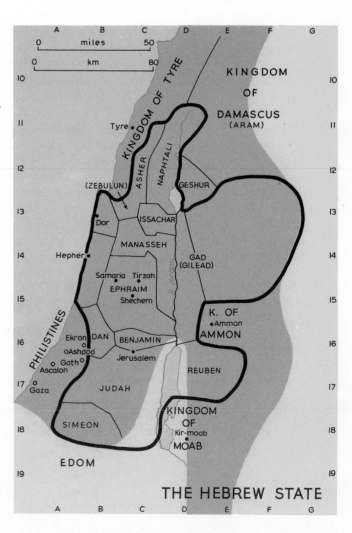

THE HEBREW STATE

Ionia and Freedom 700 BC

The Greeks lived in what are called "city-states." They were not cities in our sense: the vast majority were only fortified villages with a few thousand inhabitants farming the land within a day's walk. But they were states. The Greek got his nationality from the city of his birth and his patriotism was for his city.

Neighbouring cities often formed a league for defensive purposes and there was a general feeling that Greeks should stick together against non-Greeks (whom they called "barbarians"). However, this could not be relied on: Greek city-states were as likely to attack each other as help each other.

In the eighth century BC the Greeks of Greece were outshone by the Greeks of west Anatolia and its offshore islands. The settlements there, which dated from the period of upheaval at the end of the Bronze Age (p. 34), were particularly successful in the Ionian, or central, area. The twelve Ionian cities belonged to a league whose officials met at a temple called "the Pan-Ionium." This was on the site of a thirteenth city, Melie, that they had all united to destroy in about 800 BC.

To the north of the Ionians were the Aeolian Greeks, to the south the Dorians. There were five Dorian cities – three on Rhodes, one on Cos, and Cnidus on its long thin peninsula. Herodotus, the first man to write a history book (c. 450 BC), says that Halicarnassus was also a Dorian city but that it had been expelled from the Dorian League for bad behaviour. But Herodotus was born in Halicarnassus and this was probably a bit of special pleading for his home town. In fact it seems to have been a Carian village that gradually became Hellenized (Greek-ized) in manner and, to a lesser extent, in population.

Relations between the Greeks and the natives (Mysians, Lydians and Carians) started off well. All Anatolia was in theory part of the Phrygian kingdom which had its capital at Gordium. The Phrygians were not very interested in their western coastline and made no effort to impose their suzerainty on the Greeks. The locals took their cue from the Phrygians. Then about 680 a horde of Cimmerians from the Russian steppe broke through the Caucasus Mountains into Anatolia and overthrew the Phrygian kingdom.

The Lydians now founded a kingdom of their own with its capital at Sardes. Independence made them much more aggressive and they began to attack the mainland Greek cities. Up to about 550 they had little success but in the period 550–525 King Croesus of Lydia conquered the whole coastline.

Even in their best days the Ionians were not of much importance in military or political terms. But history is more than a catalogue of empires and Ionia marks a great step forward in social organization. Democracy started there, with freedom of speech and thought.

Two inventions – the alphabet and money – provided the basis for this new society. The alphabet was so much simpler than all other systems of writing that the peoples who used it quickly became more literate and intelligent than their contemporaries. Money gave the successful man independence and the confidence to speak his mind: the able could work for themselves instead of hoping for the favor of the great.[1]

We know that it was the Lydians who invented money (about 700), and the alphabet appears as early in Phrygia as it does on the coast (about 800) but the Greeks were able to remake their society while the inland peoples never did. This is because the Greeks were seafarers and therefore able to take advantage of the rise in trade that accompanied these innovations. It is worth remembering that until the railroad came, water was the only means of moving goods at a reasonable cost. So seafaring peoples were usually ahead in economic and social progress.

[1] It is often said that the Phoenicians invented the alphabet and there is some truth in it: it is a matter of how you define an alphabet. As we have seen, new syllabaries came into use during the second millennium BC in which only consonant-vowel combinations were represented (p. 32). And the Egyptians, remember, left out most of the vowels in their hieroglyphic script (p. 19). Put these two methods together and you have a system in which you need only one sign to represent the range of sounds ma me mi mo mu. An m stands for all five combinations of m+vowel. This means, in effect, an alphabet of consonants.

This is a workable way of writing – wrkbl, bt nt s clr s rl lphbts. It was the Greeks who added the vowels and created an unambiguous alphabet of the type we use today.

35 Coins of Croesus of Lydia and (36) of the Ionian town of Phocaea. Both are made of electrum, a gold-silver alloy that is found in Anatolia and was used for all the earliest coinages.

The inscription is an early Greek one. It reads from right to left but uses exactly the same sort of alphabet as we do.

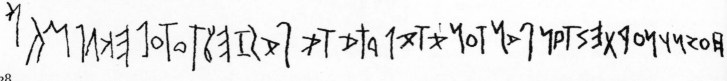

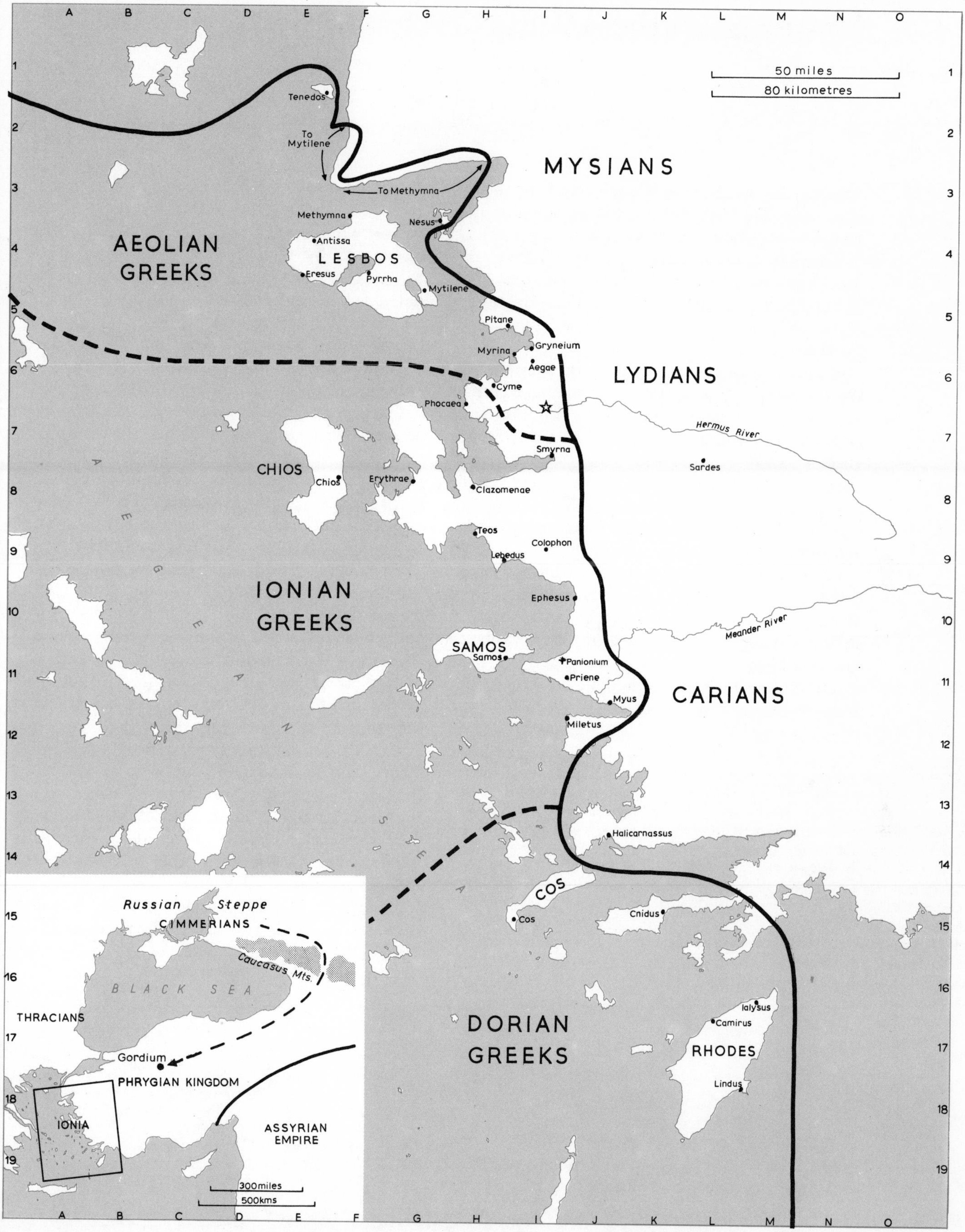

50 miles
80 kilometres
MYSIANS
LYDIANS
CARIANS
AEOLIAN GREEKS
IONIAN GREEKS
DORIAN GREEKS
LESBOS
CHIOS
SAMOS
COS
RHODES
Tenedos
To Mytilene
To Methymna
Methymna
Antissa
Eresus
Pyrrha
Mytilene
Nesus
Pitane
Myrina
Gryneium
Aegae
Cyme
Phocaea
Smyrna
Hermus River
Sardes
Chios
Erythrae
Clazomenae
Teos
Colophon
Lebedus
Ephesus
Meander River
Samos
Panionium
Priene
Myus
Miletus
Halicarnassus
Cos
Cnidus
Ialysus
Camirus
Lindus
Russian Steppe
CIMMERIANS
Caucasus Mts.
BLACK SEA
THRACIANS
Gordium
PHRYGIAN KINGDOM
IONIA
ASSYRIAN EMPIRE
300miles
500kms

☆
There were six Aeolian "cities" on the Lower Hermus: Larissa, Neonteichus, Tamnus, Cilla, Notium and Aegiroessa. Their exact sites are uncertain.

The east Mediterranean is not well off for metals: soon after the Iron Age began sailors started to search westward for new sources of supply.

The first to be successful were the Phoenicians – the people of the five Lebanese seaports Arad, Byblos, Beirut, Sidon and Tyre. They discovered silver in Tartessus in south Spain just before 1000 BC.

The next important discovery was made by the Greeks some 250 years later. They made contact with the Etruscans of central Italy who had rich deposits of iron and copper. At the same time the Greeks sailed through the Black Sea to Transcaucasia. But this was only a new way to old mines: the Transcaucasians had been supplying the Near Eastern markets with metal since Bronze Age times.

Both Phoenicians and Greeks established settlements at strategic points along their routes. These served as ports of call for trading ships and as strongpoints to protect the sea traffic from pirates and intruders.

The Euboean Greeks, who pioneered the traffic with Etruria, founded colonies at Ischia and Cumae in central Italy before 750 and, not long after, at Zancle and Rhegium on the straits between Sicily and Italy. The Black Sea route was discovered by Greeks from Miletus: the oldest Milesian colonies (Sinope and Trapezus) probably date back to the eighth century too. The Phoenician settlements on each side of the Tunisian-Sicilian narrows were older than the first Greek colonies by a couple of centuries (by their own account) or a couple of generations (more likely).

Though the first colonies were sited for trade reasons Greek emigrants soon had a quite different motive for leaving home. Greece had a bad overpopulation problem. So news of comparatively empty lands over the seas resulted in the emigration of thousands of Greeks who simply wanted to set up as farmers. Farming communities were already being established along the north coast of the Aegean: now the emigrants went farther afield – to the south of Italy and to Sicily in the west, to the Bosphorus and Black Sea in the east.

Neither the Phoenicians nor the Greeks controlled their colonies which were politically independent from the start. But two colonial cities did manage to create empires of their own. The leadership of Carthage was recognized by all Phoenician settlements in the west by the end of the sixth century. And in the next century Syracuse gained a similar position among the Sicilian Greeks. Indeed, under the leadership of Syracuse the Greeks were able to dominate the Sicilian natives.

Elsewhere, the Greek colonial cities remained enclaves in foreign lands, controlling only the area within a few kilometers of the walls. Their military power was almost zero.

37 Ships painted on a Greek bowl (500 BC). The ship on the left is a merchant-man – solid, fat and powered by a sail. The oars at its stern are for steering only. The one on the right is a warship, slim and light with eighteen oars a side as well as a sail. Its bow carries a bronze ram in the shape of a boar's head.

In battle the captain of a warship relied entirely on his oarsmen: his aim was to use his ram to hole the enemy's side. Because speed was essential the design was always pencil-like and packed in as many oarsmen as possible – it was common practice to put a second row of oarsmen above the first. A ship of this type was called a "bireme."

The one shown here is a sort of part-bireme, only the first six positions are doubled. Eventually the Athenians discovered how to build successful triremes with three rows of oarsmen. The trireme was the ship that won Athens her empire.

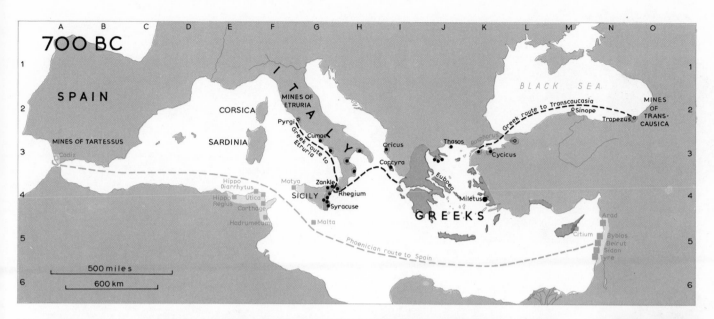

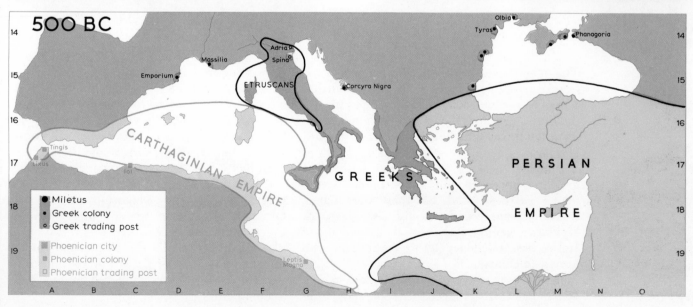

The Greeks in South Italy and Sicily

38 Metapontum (K3).

39 Sybaris (J5)

40 Syracuse (H13).

41 Acragas (D13).

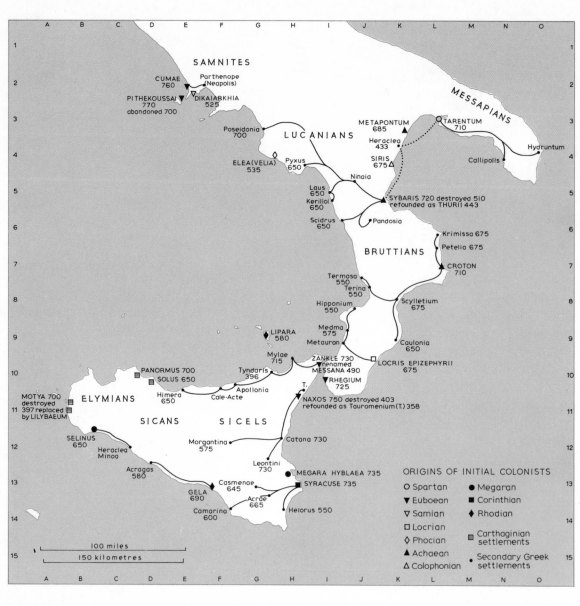

This map shows the original settlements of the Greeks in south Italy and Sicily and the further settlements founded by these colonial cities in their turn (Selinus is shown as an original settlement but it was actually founded from Megara Hyblaea).

Roughly speaking the original settlements grew to a good size while the secondary settlements remained small. But there were exceptions: Acragas became a big town, Megara Hyblaea never did. Pithekoussai on the island of Ischia was abandoned by its inhabitants who moved to Cumae.

In the early days the most famous of the Italian cities was Sybaris. Its wealth came from

the carriage of goods across the foot of Italy – a safer route than the sea voyage via the Sicilian narrows and saving the tolls charged by Zankle and Rhegium. Sybaris was destroyed in 510 by an envious Croton. Thereafter Tarentum was the biggest of the Greek colonies in Italy.

In Sicily Syracuse quickly gained first place and kept this position to the end of the Classical period. Under her leadership the Sicilian Greeks were able to beat off attacks by the Carthaginians who held the western end of the island. And gradually the Syracusans got the upper hand over the natives of the interior – something which never happened on the Italian mainland.

The Greeks in the Black Sea

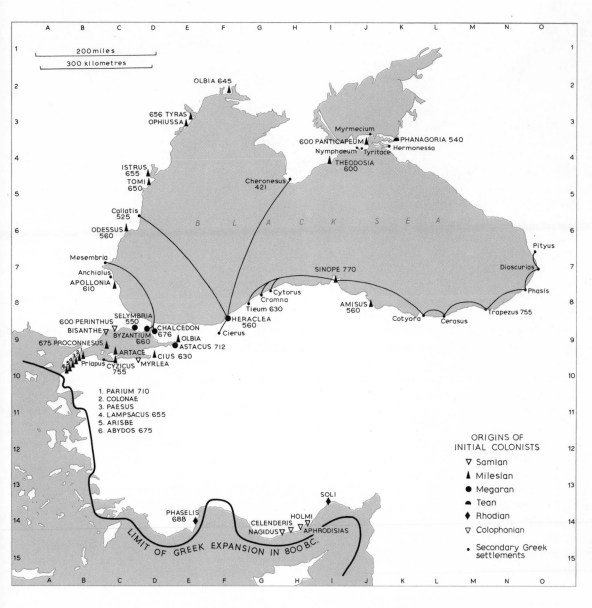

Map legend:

1. PARIUM 710
2. COLONAE
3. PAESUS
4. LAMPSACUS 655
5. ARISBE
6. ABYDOS 675

ORIGINS OF INITIAL COLONISTS
▽ Samian
▲ Milesian
● Megaran
⬣ Tean
◆ Rhodian
▽ Colophonian
• Secondary Greek settlements

42 Trapezus (N8).

43 Sinope (I7).

44 Cyzicus (C10).

45 Lampsacus (A10).

The trade route to Transcaucasia always remained in the hands of Miletus' first colony, Sinope. Sinope founded and kept control over a string of secondary colonies of which only Trapezus was of any size.

Most of the original Black Sea colonies claimed to be founded by Miletus but Megara was responsible for the cluster round the Thracian Bosphorus.

In the fifth century the Crimean cities of Theodosia, Panticapeum and Phanagoria united to form a state that became known as the Kingdom of the Bosphorus (Bosphorus means "strait." The strait between Byzantium and Chalcedon was called "the Thracian Bosphorus," that between Panticapeum and Phanagoria "the Cimmerian Bosphorus." Today Bosphorus always means the Thracian Bosphorus).

On the south coast of Anatolia there are two groups of Greek colonies – those made in the Early Iron Age upheaval and those established some 400 years later when Greek colonizing was at its height. Of the old colonies, those in Pamphylia survived to the second period but those in Cilicia had lost their Greek character by then. In the second period new colonies were founded on either side of Pamphylian towns but the Greeks were not strong enough to penetrate farther east.

43

46 Persian cavalryman.

Of the two allies who overthrew Assyria – the Medes and Babylonians – the Babylonians did better. The Medes kept Assyria itself but this was an exhausted area that never became important again. Nebuchadnezzar of Babylon took the much richer provinces of Syria and Palestine (map B).

Cyaxares, King of the Medes, made up for the unequal division by expanding in other directions. To the west he conquered Armenia and Cappadocia (but was checked by the Lydians), to the east he imposed his rule on the Hyrcanians and Parthians.

Cyaxares left the Empire to his son who lost it to the Persian king Cyrus. Persians and Medes were of the same race and this was really only a change of dynasty. Cyrus began a new bout of expansion. He conquered Lydia in the west (547), the Oxus-Jaxartes region[1] in the east (in the late 540s) and finally Babylon and its dependencies (539). The Empire was now bigger than any in the world before.

The range and success of these wars show that the plateau Iranians had learnt well the techniques of cavalry warfare taught them by the Scyths. But they still could not quite match the Scyths themselves: Cyrus the Great was finally killed in a skirmish with a minor Scythian tribe beyond the Jaxartes.

Cyrus' son Cambyses conquered Egypt in 525. The Empire now extended to its natural frontiers in all directions (map C). The next king, Darius, determined on still more conquests. He advanced through the Khyber Pass and established a province called "India." This consisted of part of the Indus River Valley – hence the name, which only later became the name for the whole sub-continent.

Then, at the other end of his empire he crossed into Europe. An expedition against "the Scyths beyond the Bosphorus" failed but Thrace was made a province and the farthest north of the Greek states, the kingdom of Macedon, was forced to pay tribute. At this moment the Ionian Greeks, under Persian control since Cyrus' conquest of Lydia, rose in revolt and the Persians had to spend the years 499–494 putting them down. In 490 came the first move against the Greeks of Greece proper and the beginning of a war that was to last, on and off, for the next 150 years.

The large map opposite shows the Empire of Darius on the eve of his attack on Greece. It is based on the lists of "satrapies" (provinces) in his inscriptions. The lists include the peoples within the dotted border along the northern edge of the Empire but it is unlikely that they paid more than occasional and token tribute.[2]

[1] These rivers are now called by their Turkish names – Amu Darya, Syr Darya. The region is part of the USSR.
[2] The Greeks, who tended to think in terms of city-states, usually referred to Lydia as the Satrapy of Sardes and to the Bosphorus province as the Satrapy of Dascylium.

47 Tribute-bearers from the satrapies of the Empire arriving at Persepolis.
Pointed-hat Scyths bring clothes, gold necklaces and a horse. Sogdians bring a pair of rams, cloth, animal skins and cups. Ionians offer beehives, cloth and cups and Cappadocians clothing and a horse. Each group is led by a court official, either a Mede (round hat) or a Persian (square hat). Frieze from the Palace of Persepolis.

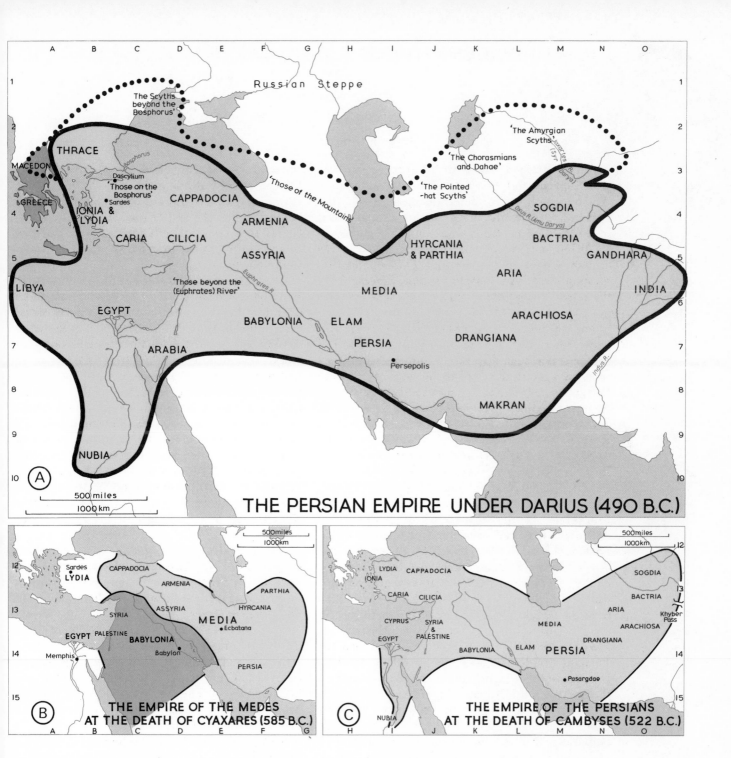

Russian Steppe

The Scyths
beyond the
Bosphorus'

'The Amyrgian
Scyths
(Jaxartes (Syr

'The Chorasmians
and Dahae'

'The Pointed
-hat Scyths'

'Those of the Mountains'

THRACE

MACEDON

GREECE

Bosphorus

Dascylium
'Those on the
Bosphorus'
Sardes

CAPPADOCIA

SOGDIA

Oxus R. (Amu Darya)

IONIA &
LYDIA

ARMENIA

BACTRIA

CARIA   CILICIA

ASSYRIA

HYRCANIA
& PARTHIA

GANDHARA

ARIA

LIBYA

'Those beyond the
(Euphrates) River'

Euphrates R.

MEDIA

INDIA

EGYPT

BABYLONIA   ELAM

ARACHIOSA

Indus R.

ARABIA

PERSIA

DRANGIANA

• Persepolis

MAKRAN

NUBIA

(A)

500 miles
1000 km

THE PERSIAN EMPIRE UNDER DARIUS (490 B.C.)

Sardes
LYDIA

CAPPADOCIA

500miles
1000km

ARMENIA

PARTHIA

SYRIA
ASSYRIA

HYRCANIA

EGYPT   PALESTINE
Memphis

BABYLONIA

MEDIA
• Ecbatana
Babylon

PERSIA

(B)

THE EMPIRE OF THE MEDES
AT THE DEATH OF CYAXARES (585 B.C.)

500miles
1000km

LYDIA   CAPPADOCIA
IONIA

SOGDIA

CARIA

BACTRIA

CILICIA

ARIA

CYPRUS   SYRIA
&
PALESTINE

MEDIA

ARACHIOSA

Khyber
Pass

EGYPT

BABYLONIA   ELAM

PERSIA

DRANGIANA

NUBIA

• Pasargdae

(C)

THE EMPIRE OF THE PERSIANS
AT THE DEATH OF CAMBYSES (522 B.C.)

Persia invades Greece 490 – 479 BC

48 Greek hoplite.

The two strongest states in fifth-century Greece were Sparta and (very much in second place) Athens. Both were determined to resist the Persians. On the other hand Thebes (Athens' rival in central Greece) and Argos (Sparta's enemy in the Peloponnesus) were pro-Persian. Macedon was already a Persian satellite and Thessaly tending the same way, so a Persian army advancing from the north would find as many friends as enemies in the peninsula.

But the first Persian attack did not come this way. Athens and Eritrea (a city on the island of Euboea) had sent help to the Ionians when they rebelled against the Persians in 499–494. So the Persians decided to send an expedition across the Aegean to punish these two cities. It set out from Samos in 490, sailed through the eastern chain of Aegean islands (which were made part of the Satrapy of Sardes) to Carystus at the south end of Euboea. Carystus surrendered, Eritrea was taken by storm. Their job half done, the Persians crossed over to the mainland and landed at the plain of Marathon on the east coast of Attica. The Athenians marched over the hills to meet them. Persians had never had much trouble in beating Greeks before because Greeks at this time had neither cavalry nor archers: on level ground they were easy game for the Persian cavalry. But this time the Greeks refused to leave the foothills and the Persians were not going to attack them there.

For several days neither side moved. Then the Persians decided to break the deadlock by shipping part of their army round the coast to make a direct attack on Athens. Their main force was moved forward to pin the Athenians to their position in the foothills while the striking force embarked. The Athenian general Miltiades took his only chance and ordered an attack. With only a few hundred yards to go the Greek army was on the Persians almost immediately. At close quarters the armored Greek spearmen were more than a match for their opponents. The battle was a massacre: 6400 Persian dead against a mere 200 Greeks.[1]

Ten years after the Battle of Marathon the Persians invaded Greece again and this time everything was carefully planned. King Xerxes led his whole army (about 60,000 strong) round the north of the Aegean. A large fleet kept pace with the army and supplied it. Thessaly fell without a fight but the Spartan king Leonidas blocked the coast road at Thermopylae with a 7000-man force that was supposed to hold until the main Greek army came up. The Persians outflanked him by slipping through the hills. While Leonidas with a rearguard of 300 Spartans stayed behind to die, the rest of the Greeks retreated as fast as they could. The Thebans (who had been coerced into fighting in the first place) went over to the enemy.

The next – and last – line of defense was at the Isthmus of Corinth. (The Athenians had had to abandon their city: they managed a fairly orderly evacuation to the offshore islands of Salamis and Aegina, and to Troezen on the mainland opposite.) Xerxes decided against a direct assault on the Isthmus, realizing that command of the sea was the key to the situation. If he could defeat the Greek navy he could outflank the Isthmus defense line as easily as he had Thermopylae. The Persians had been more successful than the Greeks in the naval engagement that took place at the same time as Thermopylae, but when the fleets met again in the narrow channel between Salamis and the mainland the Greeks won. Discouraged, Xerxes went home taking half the Persian army with him.[2]

In the next year's campaign (479) the Greeks swept the board. The Spartans led the army of the free Greeks (about 40,000 men) north from the Isthmus and met the Persians and Thebans (about the same number) near Plataea. The Persian cavalry cut in behind them, disrupted their supply lines and forced them to retreat. As the Greek army fell back the Persians pursued, but between two lines of hills they were caught without room to manœuvre. The Spartans charged: it was Marathon over again, but on a bigger scale. Few Persians escaped.

Meanwhile, the Greek fleet had sailed to Mount Mycale in Ionia and destroyed the remnants of the Persians' Aegean navy, withdrawn there after Salamis. From Mycale the victors sailed to the Hellespont, destroyed the pontoon-bridge Xerxes had built and cut off the Persian forces in Europe. Over the next few years these were eliminated and the entire north and east shores of the Aegean and the shores of the Bosphorus freed from Persian rule.

[1] The armies were originally about 10,000 apiece but several thousand Persians were at sea and so missed the battle.
[2] The Persians were not sailors and Xerxes' fleet was manned by Cypriot and Ionian Greeks, Egyptians and Phoenicians. The Athenians provided half the 360 ships in the free Greek fleet.

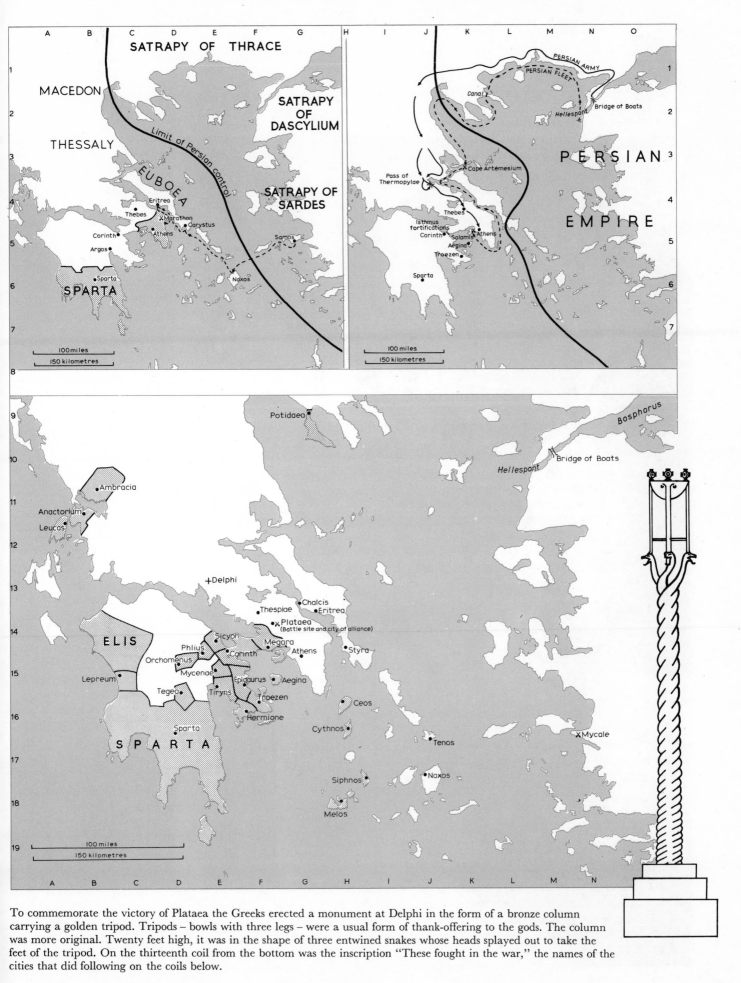

To commemorate the victory of Plataea the Greeks erected a monument at Delphi in the form of a bronze column carrying a golden tripod. Tripods – bowls with three legs – were a usual form of thank-offering to the gods. The column was more original. Twenty feet high, it was in the shape of three entwined snakes whose heads splayed out to take the feet of the tripod. On the thirteenth coil from the bottom was the inscription "These fought in the war," the names of the cities that did following on the coils below.

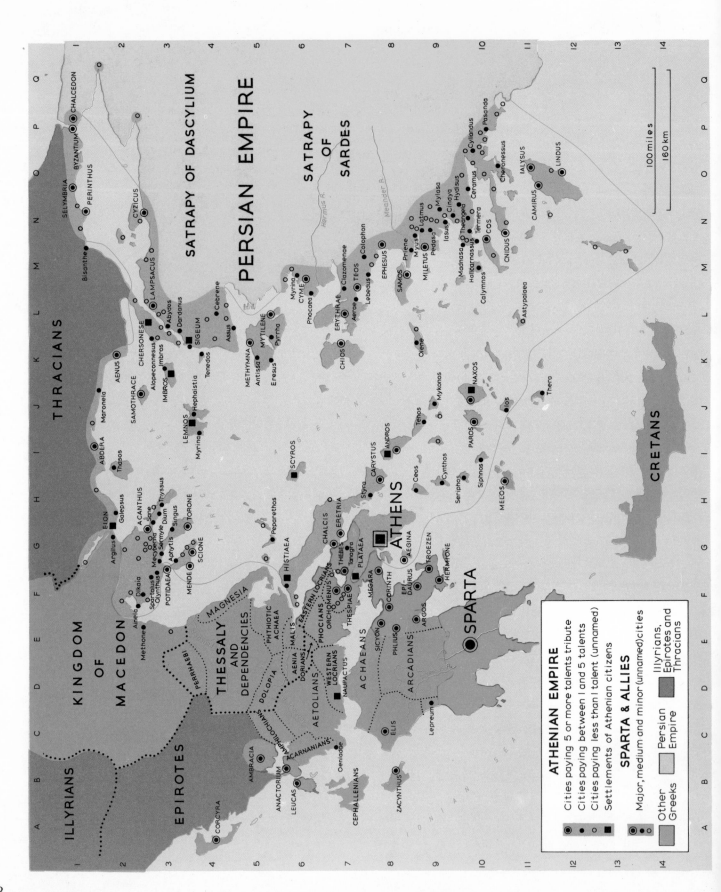

48

The Empire of Athens 479 – 404 BC

49 Greek fights Greek.

Sparta had the best army in Greece and Athens the best navy. It was the navy that freed the Greeks on the north and east shores of the Aegean so Athens ended up with an empire after the victory over Persia while Sparta got no bigger. All the liberated cities had to contribute to Athens' expenses.

The map shows the Athenian Empire twenty-five years after Xerxes' invasion of Greece. The symbols indicate the size of each particular city's contribution.[1]

The Athenian Empire lay outside peninsular Greece. Athens did try to bully her immediate neighbors and at first (mostly because Thebes was still recovering from having picked the wrong side in the Persian War) was successful in doing so. But by 447 Thebes had recovered: in that year the Athenians were expelled from Phocis, east Locris and Boeotia. A new Boeotian League with Thebes at its head took its place among the powers of Greece.[2] Next year Athens also lost control of Megara and Troezen. The collapse of Athens' land power did not much affect her strength but it left her surrounded by hostile neighbors waiting for her to blunder.

Athens' empire lasted almost to the end of the fifth century. It did not get any bigger – though this was not for want of trying. The Athenians were an aggressive, acquisitive people. Their empire ran at a profit in peacetime and whenever a fair-size treasure had accumulated a new expedition was launched. The two biggest expeditions were against Egypt and Syracuse: both were disastrous failures. Sea power was not enough for this sort of operation – even Cyprus, though conquered, could not be held – and it is typical of the Athenians that they never learned this.

As long as Athens was the only power rich enough to maintain a large navy she could afford such mistakes. She could even afford to irritate the Spartans (which she did). However, in 412 the Persians offered the Spartans the money to build a comparable fleet. Greeks may have had to swallow hard to take Persian money but by this time everyone was tired of the Athenians.

At first the Persians had to keep paying while the Spartans learnt the hard way how to fight at sea. They lost two fleets in four years. Then their admiral Lysander surprised the Athenian fleet drawn up on the beaches of Aegospotamai (opposite Abydos in the Hellespont: L3) and destroyed it. Control of the Hellespont and Bosphorus was vital to Athens: the city had outgrown the local food supply and had to import its wheat from the Black Sea region. Now with its fleet gone Athens was quickly starved into surrender. The Empire was dissolved, the Persian King getting mainland Ionia back as the price of his support.

As a great power Sparta did not long survive Athens. In 371 her army was crushingly defeated by the Thebans who then invaded the Peloponnesus and re-established Messene as an independent state.

Messene (the farthest west of the three prongs of the Peloponnese) had been conquered by the Spartans at the end of the eighth century. Sparta's position as the most powerful Greek state depended on the possession of Messene and collapsed as soon as Messene was freed. The Thebans organized an effective league among the Arcadians to make sure that Sparta would never get Messene back.

[1] Lesbos and Chios contributed ships not money. Their symbols are estimates, as are the symbols for Athens' enemies. In the case of the Boeotian League the estimate is based on the number of votes each city had.

[2] On the map, Plataea is shown as a settlement of Athenian citizens which is incorrect: the Plataeans were free allies of the Athenians. However a square symbol comes nearer the truth than a round one – which would mean they were tribute-paying subjects of the Empire. In 427 when the city was destroyed by the Thebans the refugee Plataeans were in fact granted Athenian citizenship.

Athens 500 – 320 BC

50 Athenian hoplite.

Like many other Greek cities Athens started as a hilltop settlement. This "high town" ("acropolis" in Greek) was all there was to Athens in the Bronze Age.

Probably only a few hundred people lived there then, the rest of the Athenians – meaning inhabitants of Attica – living in villages or isolated farmstead spread over the rest of the peninsula. They would have visited the clan center only for special ceremonies and assemblies.

Most Athenians were still living in the countryside when the Persians invaded but by that time there was a real town at the foot of the acropolis. This had no wall and could not be defended and though the acropolis had a wall and was defended the Persians took it by storm. Consequently, when the city was liberated, the first thing the Athenians did was to set about improving their defenses. Besides a wall round the lower city they built two parallel "long walls" that connected Athens with the port of Piraeus 6 kilometers away. Behind these fortifications the Athenians could sit out a siege by the superior Spartan army.

Athens was a democracy: all free adult male citizens had the right to vote in the assembly. Of course few could spare the time to vote on every issue so day-to-day business was delegated to a "council of 500."[1]

The assembly ("agora" in Greek) originally met at the foot of the acropolis then, as the city grew, in an open space on the northwest. Here the law courts and the chambers and offices of the council of 500 were built. The site also served as a marketplace. In time the name "agora" came to mean the place, not the assembly, and it was the place that kept the name when the assembly moved to a new open-air auditorium on the Pnyx Hill.

In the fourth century there were about 150,000 people in Attica of whom perhaps 50,000 lived in the Athens-Piraeus complex. Some 25,000 men would have had the right to vote in the assembly, though anything above 5000 would have been a very good attendance. No other Greek state had anything like as many voting citizens though some (Sparta, Thessaly and Macedon) had twice as many inhabitants.

[1] The primitive Greek system of government divided responsibility between a king, a council of nobles and an assembly of the people. In nearly all Greek states the king disappeared or became purely ceremonial (Macedon is an exception) and most came to be ruled by the council of nobles. These states are called "oligarchies," meaning "ruled by the few."

In addition to the council of 500 Athens had a council of the oligarchic type which met on the areopagus (Hill of Mars). It acted as a sort of supreme court.

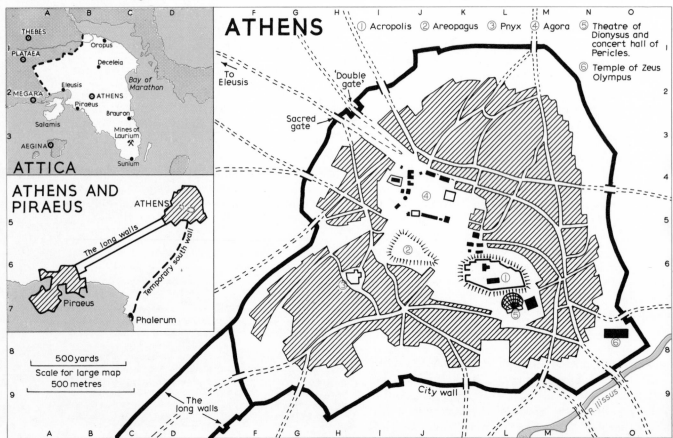

ATTICA

THEBES
PLATAEA
Oropus
Deceleia
Eleusis
Bay of Marathon
MEGARA
ATHENS
Piraeus
Brauron
Salamis
Mines of Laurium
AEGINA
Sunium

ATHENS AND PIRAEUS

ATHENS
The long walls
temporary south wall
Piraeus
Phalerum

500 yards
Scale for large map
500 metres

ATHENS

① Acropolis ② Areopagus ③ Pnyx ④ Agora ⑤ Theatre of Dionysus and concert hall of Pericles.
⑥ Temple of Zeus Olympus

To Eleusis
'Double gate'
Sacred gate
City wall
The long walls
R. Ilissus

51 A model of the Athenian Acropolis. The acropolis was reserved for ceremonial buildings in the Classical period. The Persian invasion of 480 destroyed the original temples: by the time the Athenians began serious rebuilding (447) they had conquered an empire and were able to do the job on a grand scale.

Other Greeks built their temples in stone; for the Acropolis the Athenians used marble throughout. Other Greeks fashioned their gods in bronze; Athena's cult-image was of ivory and gold. The new buildings were meant to impress and, battered though they are today, they still do.

Athena, patron goddess of the city, was the central object of all the glorification. The main temple, the Parthenon, was dedicated to her as a virgin (Athena Parthenos). A 30-foot bronze statue of her as a warrior (Athena Promachos) stood in the center of the area (the gold and ivory statue was inside the Parthenon).

The Parthenon was completed in the 430s; work then started on the Propylaea. This is the monumental gateway at the top of the entrance ramp. The little temple on the bastion on the far side of the ramp was built about 425. It was dedicated to Athena the Victorious (Athena Nike). The last years of the Empire saw the building of the irregular temple on the left of the Parthenon, the Erechtheum. Erechtheus was the legendary founder of the city.

The buildings between the Parthenon and the Propylaea are the Chalcotheca (a storehouse for weapons) and a precinct sacred to Artemis of Brauron.

The walls of the Acropolis go back to the Bronze Age but were altered and repaired many times. In the reconstruction that followed the Persian attack column-drums from the old Temple of Athena were used as reinforcement – they can be seen halfway up the wall on the left-hand side of the model.

52 The Athenian Agora. A model of the public buildings on the west sides.

The round building on the left is the official residence of the President of the Council of 500: the Council met in the two-story building behind. The colonnaded building to the right, the Metroon, is partly a temple dedicated to the Mother of the Gods, partly a storehouse for the State records. The last building in the line is the Stoa of Zeus.

The Temple of Hephaestos which over-looks all these buildings is the only one still in existence.

A stoa was a colonnaded walk where people could meet in a comfortable shade. There were several more on the other side of the Agora. The Agora courtrooms, simple open-air structures, were on the north and south sides.

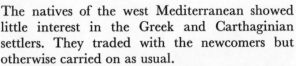

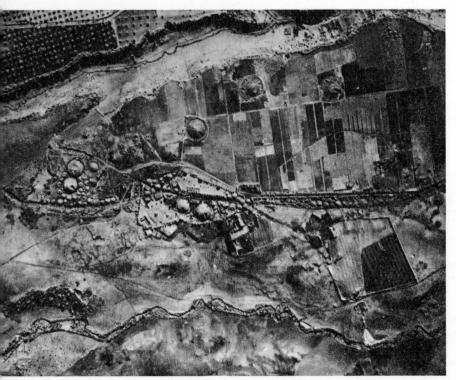

53 Etruscan soldier.

The natives of the west Mediterranean showed little interest in the Greek and Carthaginian settlers. They traded with the newcomers but otherwise carried on as usual.

The Etruscans of central Italy were an exception: their response was vigorous and intelligent. They adopted the Greek alphabet, their tribes evolved into twelve city-states on the Greek model. Indeed, the Etruscans showed an enormous appetite for things Greek and bought Greek goods at a great rate. Many of the best specimens of Greek work in our museums were found in Etruscan tombs. These imports were paid for by the Etruscan metal-mining industry.

The Etruscans were the first natives of the West to accept the idea of civilization. They were so far ahead of the others that until recently it was thought they must have come from the East. Their

Nothing remains today of the Etruscan towns except their burial grounds. At different periods, different styles of tomb were fashionable. Between the seventh and fifth centuries BC the most common was the tumulus – a mound of earth on a circular stone base with a corridor on one radius forming the burial chamber. 54 A vertical air photograph of the cemetery of Caere (modern Cerveteri) showing a cluster of tumuli. The spokes visible on the larger tumuli are formed by the collapse of their burial chambers. The larger tombs have several because new vaults were tunnelled in when the original one was full.

The mottled appearance of the fields shows that once the whole area was covered with tumuli. Over the centuries most of them have been levelled by local farmers.

origins were said to be in Lydia.

Not many people believe this now but the Etruscans remain a rather mysterious people. Though they wrote in the Greek alphabet we cannot understand their writing. We almost certainly could if Etruscan was an Indo-European language, so it looks as though the Etruscans belong to the pre-Indo-European peoples of Europe. The only survivors of this group today are the Basques of north Spain. If we are ever to learn more about pre-Indo-European Europe, we shall have to learn to read Etruscan.

In the sixth century the Etruscans started to plant "colonies" outside Etruria. These were run by Etruscans, but locals made up most of their population. Rome, in the Latin territory round the Lower Tiber, is a typical example: the kings were Etruscan but the people Latin.

Etruscan colonization ran south, along the coast, and north-east across the Apennines into the Valley of the Po. The most important of the southern colonies was Capua which soon rivalled the nearby Greek city of Cumae. The foundations in the Po Valley include many of the cities famous in Italian history – Bologna, Ravenna, Mantua and possibly, under the name Melpum, the most famous of all, Milan.

About 535 the Etruscans quarrelled with the Greeks and turned them out of their main trading post at Pyrgi in the territory of Caere. The Etruscans then formed an alliance with the Carthaginians and the two forced the Greeks out of Alalia, a colony planted a generation before on Corsica. This was the Etruscans' highpoint. Shortly after 500 they failed disastrously in an attempt to take Cumae. The people of Rome then expelled their Etruscan kings and declared the city a republic. Thereafter it was only a matter of time before the Etruscan colonies to the south were taken over by their natives too.

In the Po Valley Etruscan power did not last much longer. In 400 a wave of Gauls (Celts) swept through the Alpine passes into northern Italy. They not only seized all the cities north of the Apennines but settled there permanently. They raided Etruria itself and one successful raid went right down to Rome.

The sack of their city by the Gauls was an early humiliation the Romans always remembered. They had just wiped out the nearest Etruscan city, Veii, and the sudden swing from victory to defeat was bitter. But the Romans did not lose heart: Rome was rebuilt bigger and stronger than before.

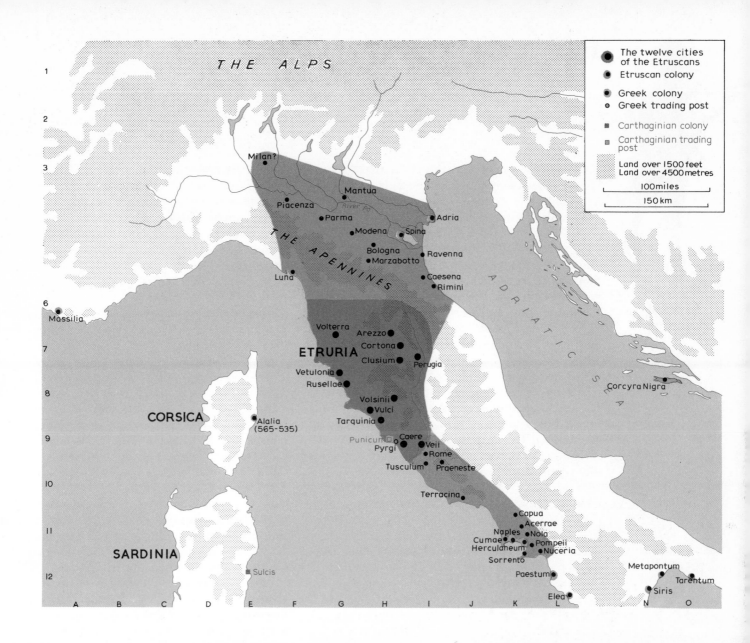

THE ALPS

Milan?

Mantua

Piacenza

Parma   River Po   Adria

Modena   Spina

Bologna   Ravenna
Marzabotto

Luna   Caesena
Rimini

THE APENNINES

Massilia

Volterra   Arezzo

ETRURIA   Cortona

Clusium   Perugia

Vetulonia

Rusellae

CORSICA   Volsinii

Alalia   Vulci
(565-535)   Tarquinia

Punicum   Caere
Pyrgi   Veii
Rome
Tusculum   Praeneste

Terracina

SARDINIA

Sulcis

Corcyra Nigra

ADRIATIC SEA

Capua
Acerrae
Nola
Naples
Cumae   Pompeii
Herculaneum   Nuceria
Sorrento
Metapontum
Paestum   Tarentum
Elea   Siris

Legend:
- The twelve cities of the Etruscans
- Etruscan colony
- Greek colony
- Greek trading post
- Carthaginian colony
- Carthaginian trading post
- Land over 1500 feet / Land over 4500 metres

100 miles

150 km

55 Group of three medium-sized tumuli from the cemetery at Caere.

India 2000 - 320 BC

56 Slave girl from Mohenjo-daro.

Before archaeology taught us better, Indian history was thought to begin with the Aryan invasion.

The Aryans were a warlike pastoral people who swept into India through the Khyber Pass about 1600 BC (p. 25). They did not begin to settle down and raise crops seriously until about 1000 BC and their first sizeable towns were only built about 700 BC. They first learnt how to write (from the Persians) about 300 years after that.

Archaeologists have found that the pre-Aryans had a level of culture far superior to that of the Aryan invaders. They lived in villages along the Indus River and its tributaries. The two biggest settlements – now known as Mohenjo-daro and Harappa – qualify as towns and were not only bigger but better built than anything the Aryans achieved in the next thousand years.

The pre-Aryans could also write. Unfortunately, the Aryans destroyed the Indus Valley settlements so completely that nothing except the faintest memory remained afterwards. And, as we cannot read the pre-Aryan script, we do not know the real names of Mohenjo-daro and Harappa nor what language their inhabitants spoke. The most popular guess is that they were Dravidians, Dravidians being the non-Aryan people who live in south India today.

By the time the Aryans did settle down they had occupied the Ganges Valley as well as the Indus region. Unlike the Indus Valley the Ganges Valley was heavily forested and the work of clearing it was a very slow business. On the other hand the land, once cleared, was exceedingly fertile.

The weight of population, therefore, began to shift from the Indus to the Upper Ganges and then to the Middle Ganges. This trend accelerated when knowledge of iron-working reached India from Persia: iron tools made forest clearance much easier.

Shortly after this the beginning of canal irrigation in the Ganges Valley gave the population there another upward push. By 400 BC there were as many Indians in the Ganges Valley as in the rest of the sub-continent. This has remained true ever since.

Hindu (Aryan) tradition says that in early times – meaning about 700 BC – there were sixteen states in the Aryan part of India, eleven of them in the Ganges Valley. The four strongest – Kosala, Malla, Licchavi and Magadha – were clustered round the Middle Ganges.

Licchavi and Malla were and remained tribal states ruled by a council of heads of clans but by 600 BC Kosala and Magadha had become monarchies. The monarchies were much more aggressive and successful than the tribal states: Kosala annexed Kashi and Magadha annexed Anga during the sixth century. In the fifth century Magadha conquered Kosala and then went on to create an empire embracing the whole Ganges Valley. Alexander's celebrated invasion of India (p. 58) never got near this Magadhan Empire which was the real India.

Besides the Magadhan Empire early Hindu society produced the first of the world's great religious figures: Buddha. He was born in the north of Kosala in the days when Kosala was still independent, indeed rather stronger than Magadha.

Tribal faiths were then weakening under the impact of the more ruthless monarchies. Religious men were withdrawing from the world into asceticism. Buddha preached a "Middle Way" between the greedy realism of the new states and the withdrawn lives of the ascetics: he wanted men to get rid of their desire for worldly gain but remain concerned with society. He wanted them above all to be charitable.

When he died at Kusinara in about 480 BC he left behind a band of disciples to carry on his teaching: over the next two centuries his ideas came to dominate the thinking of the Hindu élite. And that was only the beginning of Buddhism.

57 Seal from Mohenjo-daro decorated with a hump-backed bull and inscribed with the owner's name. The script is as yet un-deciphered but is certainly syllabic.

A thousand years after the destruction of the Indus Valley civilization the Persians reintroduced the art of writing. The new Indian scripts were based on the alphabets used by the Persians and so were consonantal.

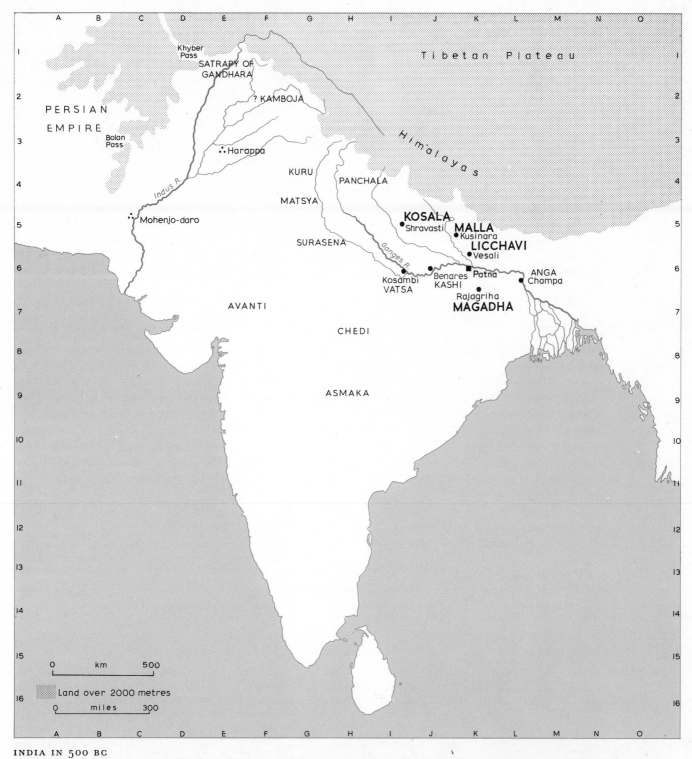

INDIA IN 500 BC

The two major sites of the Indus Valley civilization had been deserted for 1000 years by this time. Of the sixteen traditional Aryan "lands" one, Gandhara, had become a satrapy of the Persian Empire. The position of a second, Kamboja, is uncertain. Kashi, with its capital of Benares, had already been incorporated in Kosala and Anga, with its capital of Champa, in Magadha. The Magadhan capital was originally at Rajagriha but a new capital was built at Patna about the date of this map. Patna remained the capital for the rest of the Magadhan period.

The south at this time was very sparsely inhabited: the Dravidian peoples who lived there were only just beginning to change from food-gathering to agriculture.

China 1500 – 400 BC

58 Chinese warrior.

China is roughly square – bounded by the Gobi Desert to the north, the Tibetan plateau to the west and the sea to the east and south. In the Tibetan plateau rise China's two great rivers, the Hwang Ho (Yellow River) and Yangtze Kiang.[1] The Yellow River runs north into the Gobi then turns south and round the Shansi plateau to the sea. The last part of its course is level and the river has reached the sea by different routes at different times.

If you remember that *king* means "capital city," Peking (Peiking) means "north capital" and Nanking "south capital" you have half the points of the compass in Chinese: *pei* (north), *nan* (south), *si* (west) and *tung* (east). You can then work out the names of the provinces round the Lower Hwang Ho: Hopei means "north of the river," Honan, "south of the river," Shansi "west of the mountains" (*shan* means "mountains": the T'ai Hang Shan form the eastern edge of the Shansi plateau), Shantung "east of the mountains." The fifth province Shensi, is so called because it lies west of the passes (*shen*) between the Wei River and the Yellow River.

Early Chinese history, like early Chinese agriculture, is centered on these five provinces. About 1600 BC the peasants there moved into the Bronze Age and a dynasty called the Shang established a kingdom ruling most of them. In the Early Shang period the capital was at Cheng-chou but it later moved to An-yang.

The Shang kingdom was a feudal structure – with distant barons rendering only as much homage as they thought necessary. One of these baronies was the Chou state in the Wei River Valley in Shensi. In 1100 the Chou rebelled against the Shang: by 1000 Chou had won. The Chou kingdom was as loose-knit as the Shang but rather larger. It lasted from 1000 to 770 when the whole structure broke up into a hundred or more independent states of various sizes. The most important are shown on the third map. Over the next few hundred years the number of these states fell as the bigger ate the smaller. By 405 there were only thirteen left, among them a little Chou kingdom round Lo-yang.[2] But the major state of Chin then split into three, bringing the total up to fifteen in 400 BC.

The period after the collapse of Chou authority is very important: in it China moved into the Iron Age (about 500 BC), her agriculture expanded to include the Yangtze Valley (growing rice, not wheat as in the Hwang Ho Valley) and the population rose steadily (from something like 5 million to about 20 million). The major Chinese states also began to evolve a special sort of bureaucracy based on a high educational standard. The credit for this system is traditionally given to Confucius who was adviser to the Duke of Lu about 500 BC.

Two other innovations came right at the end of the period. About 450 the state of Ch'i built a wall to protect its south frontier. And at much the same time the state of Ch'in in Shensi made the first experiments in irrigation by canals. Both building walls and cutting canals grew enormously in the next two centuries. They reflect the change-over from a feudal to a centralizing society: from the warrior lord to the scholar bureaucrat.

[1] Both Ho and Kiang mean "river." The name Yangtze Kiang, which means "the river of Yang village," was popularized by the English in the nineteenth century. The Chinese only use it for a short stretch near the river's mouth. They call the Yangtze Kiang the Ch'ang Kiang (Long River) or Ta Kiang (Great River).
[2] The original Chou homeland in Shensi with its capital of Chang-an had become the independent state of Ch'in.

Shang script	𛰣	𛰤	𛰥	)	𛰦
Modern Chinese script	人	虎	車	月	山
Alphabetic equivalent	jen	hu	ch'e	yueh	shan
Meaning	man	tiger	chariot	moon	mountain

The Shang Chinese must have either seen or heard of the cuneiform scripts used in the West, for their writing is a syllabary of the same type. Modern China still uses what is essentially the same script. It is the only one of the old-style syllabaries still in use.

The Shang script is not far from picture-writing: the determinatives needed to make the meaning clear were added in the Chou period (for determinatives see Egyptian Writing, page 19). The individual signs – always referred to as "characters" – were simplified at the same time. However, it was only at the very end of the Chou period when brush and ink became the normal method of writing that the script took on the brushwork quality that gives it its unique appearance.

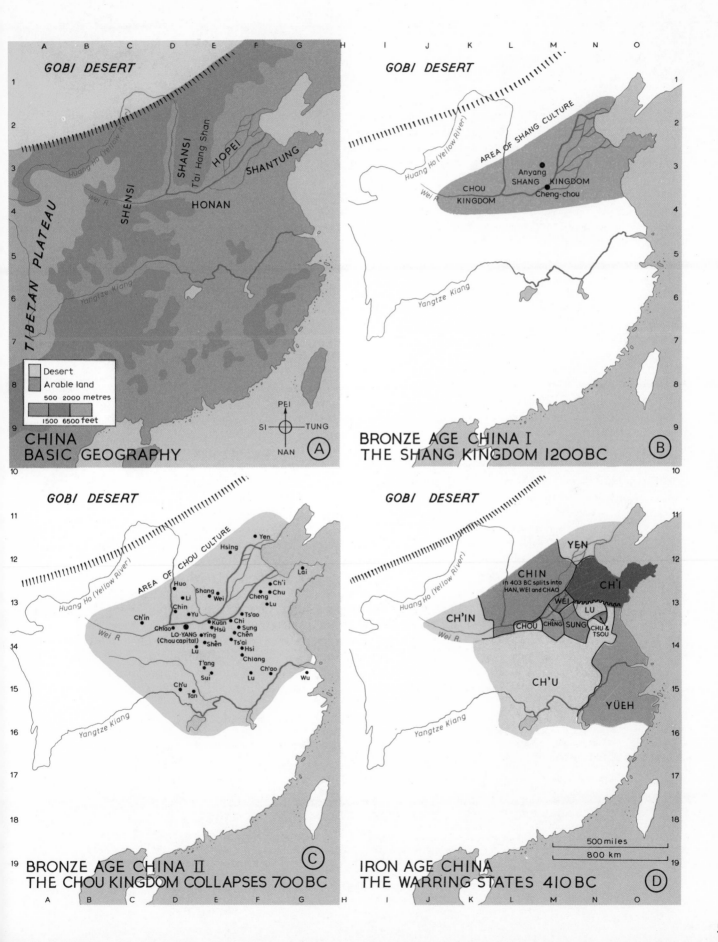

GOBI DESERT

SHANSI
SHENSI
HOPEI
T'ai Hang Shan
SHANTUNG
HONAN

TIBETAN PLATEAU

Huang Ho (Yellow R.)
Wei R.
Yangtze Kiang

Desert
Arable land
500 2000 metres
1500 6500 feet

**CHINA
BASIC GEOGRAPHY** (A)

PEI
SI — TUNG
NAN

GOBI DESERT

Huang Ho (Yellow River)
AREA OF SHANG CULTURE
Anyang
SHANG KINGDOM
CHOU
KINGDOM
Cheng-chou
Wei R.

Yangtze Kiang

**BRONZE AGE CHINA I
THE SHANG KINGDOM 1200 BC** (B)

GOBI DESERT

Huang Ho (Yellow River)
AREA OF CHOU CULTURE
Yen
Hsing
Lai
Huo
Ch'i
Shang
Chu
Li
Wei
Cheng
Chin
Yu
Lu
Ch'in
Kuan
Chi
Ts'ao
Chiao
Hsü
Sung
LO·YANG
(Chou capital)
Ying
Chên
Shên
Ts'ai
Lu
Hsi
Chiang
T'ang
Ch'ao
Sui
Lu
Wu
Ch'u
Tan
Wei R.
Yangtze Kiang

**BRONZE AGE CHINA II
THE CHOU KINGDOM COLLAPSES 700 BC** (C)

GOBI DESERT

Huang Ho (Yellow River)
YEN
CHIN
in 403 BC splits into
HAN, WEI and CHAO
CH'I
CH'IN
WEI
LU
CHOU CHENG SUNG
CHU & TSOU
Wei R.
CH'U
YÜEH
Yangtze Kiang

500 miles
800 km

**IRON AGE CHINA
THE WARRING STATES 410 BC** (D)

A B C D E F G H I J K L M N O

57

Alexander the Great 336 – 323 BC

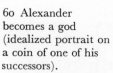

60 Alexander becomes a god (idealized portrait on a coin of one of his successors).

59 Alexander (contemporary portrait).

The stalemate between Greek and Persian was eventually broken by the one Greek state that was a kingdom. Macedon was a poor country but it was, by Greek standards, a large one – and it was run by one man.

Philip, who was its king from 359 to 336, made the Macedonian army the biggest and best in Greece. He conquered Thessaly and Thrace and extended his rule over the hill tribes behind Macedon. He then defeated the combined forces of Athens and Thebes in a hard-fought battle at Chaeronea, near Thebes, in 338. This put an end to the squabbling among the Greek city-states: they were all forced to join a Macedon-led league and to send contingents to the army Philip was assembling for the invasion of Persia.

Philip was killed by an assassin the year the war started (336) and his twenty-year-old son Alexander took over command. To show everyone that Philip's death had not changed anything, Alexander led his troops on a swift campaign through the hill country inland and then down into Greece. Thebes was trying to eject its Macedonian garrison: on Alexander's orders the city was razed to the ground.

Now he was ready for the big challenge. In 334 he marched east along the road Xerxes had taken 150 years before,[1] and shipped his army across the Hellespont. After sacrificing to the old heroes of Homeric times at the deserted site of Troy, he moved against the Persian army gathered by the satraps of Sardes, Dascylium and Cappadocia. The Persians were drawn up behind the shallow River Granicus. Alexander led his cavalry across the river and put the Persian horsemen to flight. His hoplites then made short work of the foot soldiers (they were mainly Greek mercenaries: the

Persians had long since realized that when it came to heavy infantry no Asian troops were a match for Greek hoplites). The victory won Anatolia for Alexander.

The next year he met the main Persian army under King Darius at Issus in Syria. Issus was an even more dazzling victory than Granicus. However it did not finish the war, for Alexander had to move down the coast to Egypt rather than chase Darius into Persia.

Alexander had no fleet to speak of – the army was using up all the money he had – and the only way he could defeat the Persian fleet was by taking all its bases along the Mediterranean coast.[2] This long detour gave Darius time to collect another army in Assyria and it was here – at Gaugamela – that the final battle was fought two years later (331). Darius' army was completely defeated and though he himself got away he was murdered the next year by the Satrap of Bactria.

Alexander spent the last few years of his life campaigning ever farther east – until finally in India his soldiers refused to go any farther from home and he marched back to Persia (324). He died of typhoid at Babylon the next year, still only thirty-three years old.

Alexander was a great soldier. He was also a good administrator and saw that Persians and Greeks must work together if the vast empire was to function. Though his veteran captains growled their disapproval he insisted on raising Persian units for the army and giving high posts to Persian officials.

The trouble was that he liked fighting too much: it was one thing to make a quick trip through the Khyber Pass and collect the tribute that the nearer Indus tribes traditionally gave the Persian king, it

[1] But much faster: his army took only two weeks to cover the distance between Macedonia and the Hellespont. Xerxes (going the other way) had taken three months.
[2] The sea ports all gave in without a fight except for Tyre. Tyre was built on an island 800 meters off the coast so the Tyrians were not frightened of the Macedonian army. Alexander set his men to build a causeway to the island but when it was half built the Tyrians crashed a fireship into it and it went up in smoke. The Macedonians started all over again. This time they had warships to protect them for the Cypriot and Phoenician captains in the Persian fleet were beginning to desert to the Greek side. Eventually catapults were battering at the city wall from three sides – from the completed causeway, from a Cypriot fleet to the north and a Sidonian fleet to the south. Seven months after the siege began the south wall crumbled and Alexander and the Longshields fought their way in. The causeway is the only one of Alexander's works to survive today. Silt has collected on either side of it and Tyre now lies at the end of a peninsula, the spine of which is Alexander's siegework.
[3] The Punjab ("five rivers") is the land through which the Indus and its four main tributaries flow.

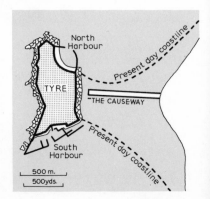

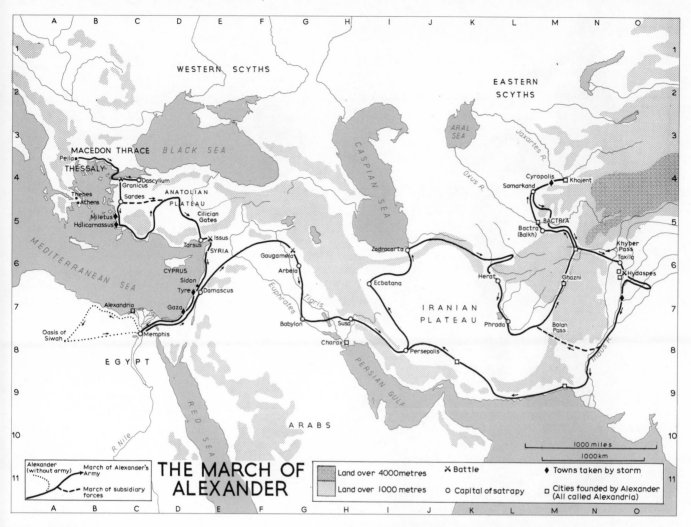

THE MARCH OF ALEXANDER

Legend:
- Alexander (without army) ·····
- March of Alexander's Army →
- March of subsidiary forces ---
- Land over 4000 metres
- Land over 1000 metres
- ✗ Battle
- O Capital of satrapy
- ◆ Towns taken by storm
- □ Cities founded by Alexander (All called Alexandria)

1000 miles
1000 km

was another to spend two years reducing the whole Punjab.[3] In fact he would have gone on to the Ganges if his soldiers had not mutinied.

What he would have got up to if he had lived, no one knows. There were rumors of expeditions planned against the Arabs, the Scyths . . . even Carthage. This restless drive was little use to his empire once he had won it, but it was part of the character of Alexander, of his intelligence and success and of the legend he left behind.

ALEXANDER'S BATTLE TACTICS

The army that Philip of Macedon created and Alexander led against Persia was exceptional for a Greek one: it had adequate cavalry. Macedon and Thessaly were the only parts of Greece flat enough to breed horsemen and they provided the heavy cavalry. The less important light horse regiments were either from Macedon or Thrace. In hilly Greece battles could be won with foot soldiers alone, but if Alexander was to win in open country he had to find cavalry to equal Persia's.

Alexander used the same tactics in all his major battles. They were based on those of Epaminondas, the Theban general who beat up the Spartans in the period 371–362. Normally, Greek hoplites simply formed a line and charged: Epaminondas showed what a devastating effect

you could have if you made one wing very strong, hit the enemy with this wing first, then crumpled up his line from this broken-up end. Alexander, facing an enemy with good cavalry, had to protect the flank of his attacking wing and he did this with a cavalry and light infantry screen. The attacking wing – always the right – was not much stronger in numbers but it contained the best regiments: the Companions (Macedonian heavy cavalry) and the Longshields (the senior of the four Macedonian hoplite regiments). Alexander led them to the attack himself, swerving inwards during the final stage to hit the left end of the enemy's infantry line.

The only disadvantage in this system was that gaps would open up between the various hoplite regiments and enemy attacks would often sail right through these. This happened at Issus and let half the enemy infantry escape and at Gaugamela where the Macedonian camp was overrun and sacked. But in both cases Alexander destroyed the center of the Persian army and won the field.

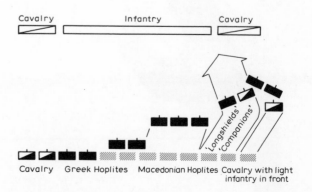

Cavalry   Infantry   Cavalry

Cavalry   Greek Hoplites   Macedonian Hoplites   Cavalry with light infantry in front

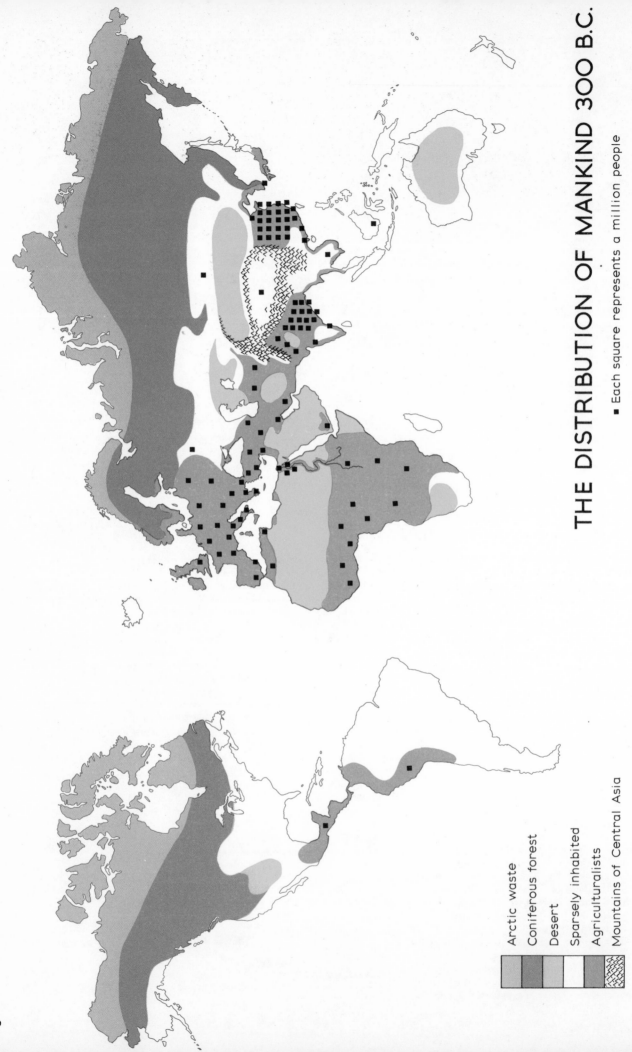

THE DISTRIBUTION OF MANKIND 300 B.C.

■ Each square represents a million people

Arctic waste
Coniferous forest
Desert
Sparsely inhabited
Agriculturalists
Mountains of Central Asia

The World at the Death of Alexander 320 BC

By 320 BC the population of the world had reached the 100 million mark.

Distribution was uneven and becoming more so. Some areas – the deserts, the Arctic tundra and the northern conifer forests – never had and never would have more than the occasional band of hunters. Other areas, though perfectly suitable for agriculture, had not yet been settled by farmers: South Africa, Southeast Asia, parts of Australasia and much of the Americas.

In the Americas farming had begun in a small way as early as 4000 BC. This was quite independent of Old World farming: the staple was Indian corn (maize) not wheat or barley. But though villages appeared in Mexico by 3000 BC their spread was very slow: in 300 BC the settled area was still limited to a strip from Mexico to Peru. Even in this strip the villages were few and far between. Altogether the New World probably had no more farmers than hunters, about a million of each.

So almost everyone lived in the Old World. Even here there were large areas where people were thin on the ground. Central Asia saw only a few nomadic herdsmen: Africa south of the Sahara had a growing but still scanty number of Negro peasant farmers; the Malays of Southeast Asia were only just beginning to farm their land and their colonization of Indonesia had barely begun.

By contrast the peasants of India and China were already teeming. The valleys of the Ganges and Indus, of the Yellow River and Yangtze Kiang held at least a third of mankind. Less dense but as large was the population of the Europe–Near East area. From the Fertile Crescent, where population was levelling off, the center of gravity of this area was shifting west. Its new axis was the Mediterranean.

China, India and the Mediterranean: these were the three worlds in which most men have lived between then and now. And through most of history the three have gone their own ways as if they were separate planets. But one thing they all had (and the other societies did not) was a small proportion of people who could read and write.

Literacy is the only sure way of passing one generation's learning to the next: in it lay the hope of escape from the brutal labor that was most people's lot. For if the quantity of human life had increased twenty times since the Neolithic revolution, the quality of human life had hardly improved at all. Half the babies born died in childhood, most of those who lived to adult life did not see forty. What was called medicine simply made being ill more unpleasant. And between diseases and disasters continued always man's inhumanity to man: cruelty was universal and unceasing.

It was to try to soften this harshness that Buddha preached his gospel of charity: his aim was to reform the individual. The Chinese philosopher Confucius took a less optimistic view of human nature but hoped for the same result through administration by a selfless élite.

In Greece Plato put forward a rather similar idea in his book *The Republic* but though widely admired it was never taken as more than a theory: there was not the same gap between rulers and ruled in Greece as existed in Asia. In many Greek states all free men had a say in affairs and, even if benevolent despotism held out the appeal of greater efficiency, most Greeks felt that democracy was a better kind of government. Even Alexander's godlike progress could not dispel the feeling that the Macedonians, because they were ruled by a king, were not a truly Greek people.

The trouble with democracy was that it worked only for small communities and small communities were always in danger of being swallowed up by bigger ones. Greek democracy only survived its conflict with Persia because of the Greek hoplite. And half the hoplites were provided by the undemocratic Spartans. In the end the Macedonian kings recruited even more hoplites and Greek freedom was confined to local government. When the Romans unified the Mediterranean world even local freedom dwindled away. A Dark Age and a Feudal Age had to pass before individual liberty appeared again.

Nevertheless, freedom was to be a key idea of Western society. In Asia, on the other hand, Buddhism and Confucianism encouraged men to accept authority and their own lot. This may have kept Asia in its unchanging routine. The West's contribution to history has been to show that the real freedom is the freedom to change. No answers are forever.

Acknowledgements for Photographs

Aerofilms 6
American School of Classical Studies at Athens 51, 52
Archives Photographiques, Paris 1, 2
British Museum, London 10–12, 14–17, 30, 33, 37, 46, 50
Brundage Collection, M. H. de Young Memorial Museum, San Francisco 58
Champollion, J. F. 22, 32 (from *Monuments de l'Egypt et de la Nubie*, 1835)
Clayton, Peter 24, 26, 35, 40
Eduard-Meyerschen-Fremdvolker-Expedition 13
Fototeca Unione, Rome 54
Frankfort, Mrs. E. 4 (from H. Frankfort, *Art and Architecture of the Ancient Orient*, 1954)
Giraudou 8

Hirmer Fotoarchiv, Munchen 5, 9, 18, 20, 23, 25, 36, 39, 41, 44, 45, 49
Hurliman, Martin 53
Italian State Tourist Office 55
Louvre, Paris 3
Metropolitan Museum of Art, New York 48
Museum of Fine Arts, Boston 19
National Museum of Pakistan, Karachi 56, 57
Oriental Institute, University of Chicago 47
Powell, Josephine 21, 27, 29
Roger-Viollet 7
Staatliche Museen zu Berlin 31, 34
Webb, John (Brompton Studio) 38, 42, 43, 59, 60
Wieszinski, W., *Atlas* 1923–35 28

Sources and Notes

p.1 Data for the gateway reconstruction will be found in Place, V. *Nineveh et Assyrie*, Paris 1867–70 and Loud, G. *Khorsabad*, II, Chicago 1938.

p.4–7 The drawings are by Edward Mortlemans. Only the major icecaps are shown on map 7; the exact limits of those in Asia and the degree to which they coalesced are uncertain.

p.12 Photo 3. Stamping an object with a seal is a good way of marking it as one's own: in societies without writing a picture serves as a signature. We still use stamp seals. In early Mesopotamia they favoured cylinder seals which could be rolled along to produce a repeating pattern. The emblems on this one are obvious choices for a farmer.

p.14 Photo 5. The spearman is one of a procession on the "banner of Ur", a shell and lapis lazuli mosaic.

p.16 In Gudea's inscription the sign for "god" was probably an unpronounced determinative of the type discussed in the section on Egyptian writing (p.19). Note that Gudea distinguishes Lagash state (Lagasa) from Lagash town (Girsu). The translation was supplied by C. B. S. Walker.

p.17 The map of Sumer is based on that in Roux, G. *Ancient Iraq*, London 1966.

p.19 Like most Egyptian inscriptions Tjetji's reads from right to left. Egyptians could write either way, the direction being shown by the way the animals faced. The translation was supplied by A. F. Shore.
Photo 15 is from a copy of a painting in one of the tombs of the nobles at Shek Abd el-Kurna (Map 28 E7). The early papyrus (Photo 16) was found in the funeral temple associated with Pharaoh Neferirkare's pyramid at Abusir; the later one (Photo 17) is part of the Great Harris papyrus.

p.21 For the architecture of the pyramids see Edwards, I. E. S. *The Pyramids of Egypt* London 1961 and Vandier, *J. Manuel*

d'Archaeologie Egyptienne, II i Paris 1954. For the ziggurat of Ur see Wooley, C. L. *Ur Excavations*, V, London 1939.

p.23 The most recent account of the nomes is in Montet, P. *Geographie de l'Egypte Ancienne*, Paris 1961. For advice on the Greek equivalents we are indebted to Russell Gore-Andrews.

p.25 Photo 21. The charioteer is carved on the gravestone of one of the shaft graves at Mycenae.

p.28 Detailed plans of the individual buildings at Luxor will be found in Vandier, *op. cit.*, II ii.

p.33 The map is based on those in Page, D. L. *History and the Homeric Iliad*, California 1959.

p.37 The map is based on Aharoni, Y. and Avi-Yonah, M. *The McMillan Bible Atlas*, New York 1968, map 113.

p.47 The Plataea memorial has an interesting later history. The tripod only survived for a little over a hundred years before being melted down to pay a Phocian army. The column remained at Delphi for a further 700 years. Then the Roman Emperor Constantine the Great took it to his new capital of Constantinople, and put it in the centre of the city's hippodrome. In 1700 A.D. the serpents' heads, which were soldered on to the main casting, fell off, but the rest of the column is still there.

p.48 The tributes exacted by Athens are itemized in Meritt, Wade-Gery and McGregor *The Athenian Tribute Lists*, Cambridge, Mass./Princeton 1939–53.

p.50 The map of Athens is based on those in Travlos *Poleodomiki exelixis ton Athinon apo ton proistorikon chronon mechri tou archon tou 19ou aionos*, Athens 1960.

p.57 Map C is based on Cheng, *Archaeology in China*, III Cambridge, England 1963: Map D on Herrmann, A. *An historical atlas of China*, Chicago 1966, p.6.

Index

This is a geographical index to the peoples and places appearing on the maps. It has no entries for the text, photographs, captions or diagrams, nor any for the maps before page 17. As the function of the index is to locate there is only one entry per name. The name is followed by a page number and then by a letter-number combination which gives a reference point inside the map on that page.

Entries in capitals have a map to themselves. Nome references after Egyptian towns refer to the tables on p. 23 and 26. Greek names that ended in -os and -on were written by the Romans as -us and -um. Except for the Greek islands the modern preference is to follow the Roman usage (Miletus, Byzantium) but the preference is not consistent and in most cases either will do.

Abbreviations:
anc. = ancient
Assyr. = Assyrian
class. = classical
Hom. = Homeric
mod. = modern
syn. = the same as
L. = Lake
R. = River